WALKING THE
SCOTTISH HIGHLANDS
General Wade's Military Roads

WALKING THE SCOTTISH HIGHLANDS

General Wade's Military Roads

Text by Michael Pollard
Photographs by Tom Ang

ANDRE DEUTSCH

The pictures are for Ros and Fay

First published in 1984 by André Deutsch Limited
105 Great Russell Street London WC1

Photographs copyright © 1984 by Tom Ang
Text copyright © 1984 by Michael Pollard
All rights reserved

Set in Van Dijck

Printed and bound in Great Britain by
Jolly & Barber Ltd, Rugby

British Library Cataloguing in Publication Data
Pollard, Michael
    Walking the Scottish highlands.
    1. Highlands of Scotland – Description and travel – Guidebooks
    I. Title II. Ang, Tom
    914.11´504858 DA880.H7

ISBN 0 233 97620 5

page 2: *Loch Lochy from the east bank*
page 6: *Near the Well of Lecht*

Contents

Maps

If you are proposing to follow the walks described in this book, you are strongly urged to obtain the relevant Ordnance Survey maps, either 1:25,000 or 1:50,000 scale. They include contours which our maps, as they are not the product of surveys, obviously cannot show

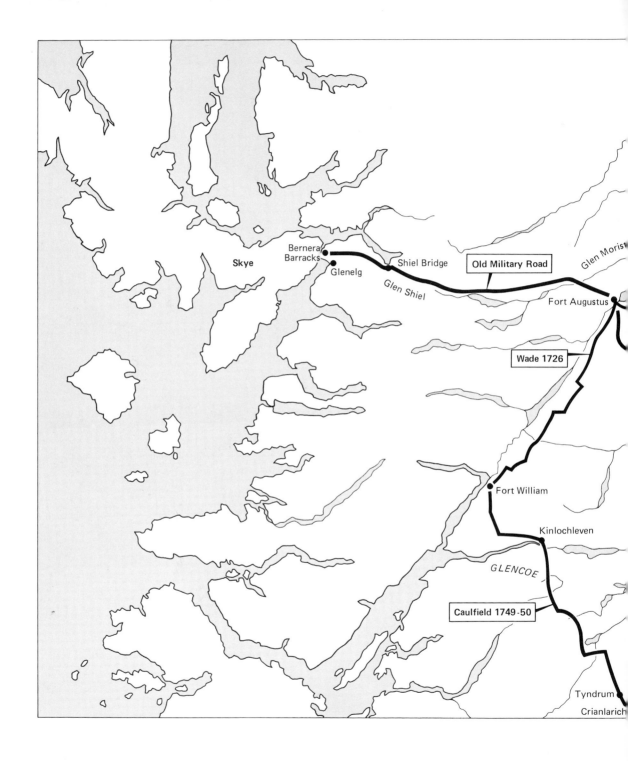

Skye

Bernera Barracks

Glenelg

Shiel Bridge

Glen Shiel

Glen Moris

Old Military Road

Fort Augustus

Wade 1726

Fort William

Kinlochleven

GLENCOE

Caulfield 1749-50

Tyndrum

Crianlarich

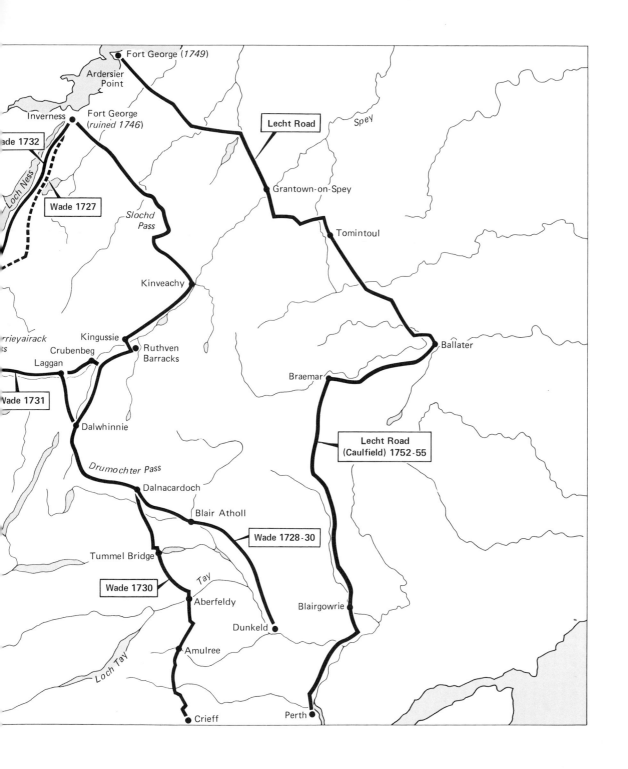

1

The King's Roads

If you are walking in Scotland anywhere between Loch Lomond and Loch Ness you are likely to find yourself following, or crossing, or walking close to something described on the map as 'General Wade's Military Road' or as an 'Old Military Road'. Some time in the 1960s this happened to me so often that my curiosity was aroused. Who was General Wade? What was he doing building roads? Why did many of them lead nowhere much, through practically uninhabited country? Why had they been allowed to decay and in some cases to disappear? What was the difference between one of General Wade's Military Roads and a military road that was merely 'Old', and how old was 'Old'? What was it all about?

To a Scot these questions will betray incredible ignorance, and I plead guilty. Like most Englishmen I knew very little of Scottish history, its study not being encouraged by English examination boards. So I did not know that for most of the eighteenth century Scotland was governed much as if it were a colonial territory, with an army of occupation to put down native uprisings, expatriate Englishmen providing a good deal of its administration and the King's flag rising and falling in front of his castles just as it was to do on the lawns of innumerable Government Houses the world over during the next century. It may be going too far to say that the tactics of nineteenth-century colonialism were worked out in the Highlands of Scotland, but there are disturbing similarities between the military government of Scotland before and after 1745 and that of parts of Africa 150 years later. In Scotland, the military road system built by Wade and others was one of the instruments of this colonialist regime.

It is only in the past century and a half in Britain, and over a shorter period in many other countries, that road-building on a national scale has become the business of local authorities and civil service departments. It is true that the Highways Act of 1555 might be considered to have set up some kind of nationwide control over roads in England and Wales, while the Turnpike Trusts of the eighteenth century took the process a little further; but the results were hardly encouraging. The effect of the 1555 Act was little more than to get a few of the worst potholes filled in by the more conscientious or resourceful parishes, while the efforts of the Turn-pike Trusts were, as contemporary travellers often noted, almost as variable. In Scotland there was from 1669 onwards a system of Statute Labour similar to that provided in England by the 1555 Act, obliging tenants to supply labour, tools, horses and carts for a number of days each year – typically, six – for road-mending purposes. The system was as unhelpful in Scotland as in England. The luckless keeper of the records – in Scotland, often the school-master – had few powers of enforcement, and if he took advantage of them he was likely to be outlawed by his community. Even in a relatively populated and unchallenging shire such as Aberdeen, it was said in 1740 that there was not one road fit for wheeled traffic.

Road networks, in Britain as elsewhere, have tended to come about in two ways: informally, through the linking of trading routes such as drove and pack roads and, more formally, as lines of communication for armies of occupation. The example of the latter category most familiar to the British is, of course, the Roman road system, which was effective enough to remain the basis of the national network in England and Wales until the motorway era, and which even now still provides a number of important arteries. But there are many instances elsewhere, including some from modern times, such as the roads of the coastal strip of North Africa, laid during the Italian and subsequently the Anglo-American occupation.

It is characteristic of military road systems that they take scant notice of whatever existed before. Armies have their own criteria and their own purposes. When the Romans built their roads in Britain they largely ignored the great prehistoric tracks like the Icknield Way and the Ridgeway. Generally, these did not lead where the armies wanted to go. What is more, the old tracks had been chosen partly for the ease with which they could be defended, and the natives were in possession. In Scotland under English rule, the situation was rather different. When the military road-builders arrived, there already existed a well-established system of drove roads converging on Crieff and Falkirk and then leading over the border country through Peebles. These were not so much roads as

The Commando Memorial,
Spean Bridge, near
Highbridge

routes, but without benefit of surveying instruments the drovers had chosen – usually from among a bleak selection – the easier passes. The army road-builders often followed the drovers, to the general displeasure of the latter who preferred unmetalled surfaces. But the coincidence of such trading routes as there were with the military roads did not prevent later critics from accusing the military of ignoring civilian commercial needs.

The Jacobite rising of 1715 forced to English attention an area of Scotland that London had, on the whole, preferred not to think about: the Highlands. The few reports that had filtered out of the region all agreed that it was a wild country inhabited by savage and apparently untameable people. Among the most savage, and indeed anarchic, were the Macdonalds of Glencoe, whose only hope of earning a living from their forlorn territory bordering the boggy Moor of Rannoch was to use it as a base from which to plunder their neighbours. The Macdonalds were the victims of the Glencoe massacre of 1692, and it may well be that, in justification of this atrocity, their characters were painted blacker than they need have been. Probably they were no better and no worse than neighbouring clans, for it is true that the Highlands in general was at times a no-go area, at other times a thieves' kitchen, and at others virtually a series of independent republics, glen by glen. Such men were beyond reach or understanding of the civilities of government as practised south of Stirling, or so it seemed, and so it was possible in 1692 for the government to distance itself from the outrage of butchering an old man, his wife and kinsmen and hunting the survivors to death through the snow, this act being performed by troops who had latterly been the Macdonalds' guests at table. The enormity of the crime was to strike home later, leading to a classic cover-up of which the legendary viciousness of the Macdonalds could have been a part; but it can be argued that the Glencoe massacre was as much a mindless blow at the intractability of the region and its people as a deliberate act against the Macdonalds themselves. But while governments can put up with lawlessness, especially in the furthermost reaches of their territories, they cannot tolerate disaffection. The events of 1714 and 1715 had made it clear that the Highlands must be secured, because the northern coasts, impossible to patrol effectively by sea, were all too vulnerable to French, Dutch or Spanish fleets bringing arms or men to aid rebellion. And the raw material for another rebellion was to hand in the glens.

The man entrusted with the security of the Highlands as Commander-in-Chief of His Majesty's Forces in Scotland from 1724 was the Irish-born General George Wade, and one of the main instruments that he chose was a road system that would, he hoped, allow the Highlands to be policed by a relatively modest force with the ability to move quickly to any trouble spot. General Wade has gone down in history (and to some extent in legend) as the creator of the first road system in the Highlands, but it is not clear how far his personal reputation is justified. He was in Scotland for thirteen years, from 1724 to 1737, and during that time saw the completion of the four roads forming the skeleton of the system, a mileage of about 250 – about a quarter of the eventual total. The work was continued over the next thirty years or so by his successors, notably by his chief surveyor William Caulfield. Wade certainly accepted responsibility for the roads built during his time in Scotland, and took a close personal interest in them, but it is far from clear how closely he was involved in their actual planning, or how far ahead he had looked when he was posted from the Scottish command in 1737. The pause of some five years that followed his departure suggests that he had not, in fact, done any forward planning, and indeed his own reports and those of Caulfield seem to indicate a fairly short time span between perceiving the need for a road, surveying the route and getting down to work. So perhaps he left his network as complete as he had intended it to be, though it is hard to believe that he intended it to end so abruptly to the west, where the road to Fort William was left out on a limb, with no direct southward connection.

Wade was a considerable public figure, the kind of man who would today be given close attention by the press and television. The eighteenth century honoured him with its closest equivalent – the writing of numerous odes and heroic addresses. As a result, later writers tended to ascribe all military roads in Scotland to him. Dorothy Wordsworth, for example, writing in 1803 within living memory of the event, has Wade building the 'Rest-and-be-thankful' road from Tarbet to Inveraray. In fact, this road was made in 1768, when Wade had been dead for twenty years. Many travel writers of the nineteenth century – and hordes of them made the journey north, under the influence of the romantic movement, to thrill to the gloom of the glens – used the term 'Wade road' for anything built before about 1800. Perhaps, as the purpose of this book is to use the military roads, or what survives of them, as a framework for walking, these are niceties that need not concern us too much; but to satisfy purists I shall use the term 'Wade roads' only for his original four, as the current Ordnance Survey does.

Some sections of the military network – notably large sections of the Dunkeld to Inverness road, now steadily being brought to trunk road standard as befits Scotland's communications spine – were later incorporated into the civilian system, and except as a means of access these are probably the least interesting sections to the walker. However, some of them also lead to sites which are of interest to anyone trying to follow the tortuous story of the Forty-Five on the ground. A handful of the forty original Wade bridges, built for the occasional traffic of horse and foot, have proved capable of withstanding the more demanding usage of our own time, while others now stand marooned and apparently irrelevant amid grass and heather. Yet other sections of the system remained in use long

Artificial lake, Spey Dam

enough to become motor roads, but have since been superseded and have quickly returned to their natural state, to the benefit of walkers. Others again, neglected earlier in their lives, have retreated still further, and can be traced only with difficulty or not at all. But what remains includes some splendid marches across country that can be reached in no other way, together with shorter stretches which are worth visiting for their intrinsic interest or can without difficulty be knitted together to make worthwhile days out.

Out of the thousand miles or so of military road which made up the system at its peak in about 1760 I have chosen six roads for close attention in this book, together with one or two brief diversions. To put the best (and most demanding) walking first, I have taken the four Wade roads in the reverse order of their construction, beginning with the challenging traverse of the Corrieyairack Pass and ending with the spinal Dunkeld to Inverness road, which is now walkable only in relatively short stretches. My last two roads are post-Wade: the route from Fort William to Crianlarich, built in 1749–50 by

Caulfield, and now designated as part of the West Highland Way long-distance footpath; and the famous Lecht Road through Tomintoul, built in 1754.

It is not always possible to follow exactly in the footsteps of Wade or his successors. Some of their roads have been overlaid by later engineering works, and some by flooding in connection with hydro-electric schemes. Sometimes all traces of their original lines have disappeared. Often, later surveyors have chosen new alignments alongside the old. I have not been such a fanatic as to take a difficult route for the sake of history when, as sometimes happens, an easier track a few yards away leads to the same end.

The world is by no means short of advice to walkers, but perhaps the special nature of the Highland terrain and climate justifies some extra comment here. I should say at the outset that I am averagely healthy but not particularly fit in any more aggressive sense. As a professional writer I lead a largely sedentary life. Walking is my most active pursuit, but I am not a dedicated or even regular long-distance walker. My record is about twenty miles in one day, which I felt at the time had been too much. I mention all this to enable the reader to gauge my judgements of a walk as punishing, arduous, reasonable or easy. In my experience there is nothing more frustrating and disheartening than to find something described in a guide-book as, say, 'an easy scramble' when in one's own terms it ranks as fairly gruelling work. Although there is nothing as demanding as a scramble on the military roads themselves, a few of my suggested excursions involve the use of hands as well as feet, but I have indicated this where appropriate. Otherwise, if you are as moderately healthy as I am, you will find no great physical challenge on the walks described in this book, unless you choose to do them in unsuitable weather or against the clock.

However, the basic rules of hill-walking apply, bearing in mind that some of these roads cross very remote and potentially hostile country. You will need stout and well-broken-in boots, thick all-wool socks, an all-wool sweater to wear and another to take in reverse, and preferably all-wool trousers. I emphasize wool because it is surprising to find how many foolhardy souls set out for the most exposed and bleak situations wearing only chain store 'leisurewear' whose manmade fabrics are magnets for every icy needle of wind. If you are walking alone, a brightly coloured anorak or cagoule is advisable, but one of these between you will suffice as a marker if you are more than one. However, in the Highlands on even the most promising day you should be equipped for rain. A spare pair of socks is useful, even on a half-day trip. As for equipment: the relevant OS map, of course, in a clear plastic envelope to protect it from the wet, a compass and a watch. A small torch and a whistle provide extra insurance, especially for the lone walker. I am not a camper, and so must leave details of camping requirements to those who know more about this form of masochism; but certainly you should not try camping in the Highlands unless you have plenty of experience behind you.

My provisions for a longish day's walk (that is, up to my famous twenty miles) would include: apples, oranges (which make particularly good eating out of doors), fruit cake, sandwiches (preferably including some with tomato or some other dampish filling) and oatcakes. These have to be packed with care, but some brands are sold in boxes containing a number of small airtight packages, and these are especially useful. Like oatcakes, dried compressed fruit of the kind sold at health food stores provides convenient bulk. It is always wise to take with you a little more food than you think you will need; apart from the possibility of being out for longer than you expect, looking forward to something to eat immensely eases a slow or difficult patch. A cyclist's plastic water bottle copes with the walker's drink problem, and on a hot day a few minutes in a stream cools it nicely.

A handful of the walks suggested in this book can be combined, with careful planning, with the use of public transport. The long West Highland Way section between Crianlarich and Fort William can be walked with the help of the West Highland Railway. The Dalwhinnie to Ruthven stretch of the Dunkeld to Inverness road has both bus and train services at each end, and the Kinveachy to Slochd section farther north need only be walked in one direction, returning by bus. Other military roads are less amenable, however, and access to starting and finishing points by car is usually essential. The hugely circuitous routes often taken in the Highlands to cover tiny distances as the crow flies rule out the usual tactic of dropping one partner at one end, driving to the other and remembering to exchange car keys halfway, and in any case the prospect of a lone walk is less appealing in this remote country than, say, on the South Downs. In

*West Highland Railway,
Tyndrum*

many cases a return journey by the same route must be accepted, and due time allowed for it. If you are going to have time to enjoy the scenery, to allow for possible uncertainties and for minor diversions, and to take reasonable breaks, you should not reckon on an average of much more than two miles an hour.

It should go without saying, but perhaps should nevertheless be said, that exploring the military roads is, for all except the most adventurous, well equipped and experienced, essentially a summer sport, from May to October inclusive. Beyond these months the days are too short, the climate, always unpredictable in the Highlands, too treacherous, and some routes are simply impassable. Even within this period you should be prepared for any kind of weather, and willing to abandon a planned walk if conditions suddenly deteriorate. It is for this reason that my earlier comments on clothing, which may seem superfluous if you are setting out on a sunny morning, are not made lightly. At the summit of the Corrieyairack, on a bright August day and despite my layers of all-wool clothing, I have felt the onset of the slowing of thought which is the first symptom of potential danger from exposure.

There is no law of trespass in Scotland, but between mid-August and mid-October there is an even more effective deterrent: the possibility of getting into the sights of a stalker or straying into the middle of a grouse shoot. In deer areas culling, using high-powered

rifles, begins in early summer. Warnings posted at access points should be carefully read and observed. The official advice to walkers, given in posters put up by the Scottish Home Department, is to inquire at the estate office, if in doubt, about the day's arrangements. You get more helpful results if you do this under the aegis of a hotel or youth hostel than if you try it from a public callbox, but in practice I have met nothing but kindness and concern from landowners and ghillies, bailiffs and shepherds, many of whom, hearing that I was writing this book, urged me to include in it a warning against reckless walking. It is justified. If you come, as I do, from a part of England where you often get the feeling that landowners are still regretting the banning of the mantrap and the spring gun, the relative freedom of Scotland can easily turn the head.

 Finally, a word for motorists. Access to the military roads, and some of the roads themselves, are often used by Land Rovers and heavy forestry equipment. Park with this in mind!

Near Melgarve

2

The General Goes North

General George Wade had a distinguished military career behind him when, at the age of fifty-one, he was posted to Scotland. He had first seen action when he was eighteen, in Flanders, and over the next twenty years saw little else, in the latter years in Spain and Portugal. In 1711 he retired with the rank of Major General and was evidently planning a quieter life, becoming Member of Parliament for a Wiltshire constituency.

With the outbreak of the Fifteen Wade returned to the colours and distinguished himself in anti-Jacobite policing operations in Bath and London, uncovering, among other things, a plot being hatched in the Swedish Embassy in London with the active support of the King of Sweden. All this evidently renewed his taste for military adventure, for in 1719 he went as second-in-command of the successful expedition to Vigo in northern Spain. After this he settled in Bath, becoming the city's MP and interesting himself in municipal good works. He had been tipped off about the Swedish plot by a postal clerk at Bath, Ralph Allen, who was presumably reading the letters that passed through his hands. Allen's reward was twofold: he was promoted to Postmaster of Bath at Wade's instigation and he was also given the hand in marriage, with a substantial dowry, of one of Wade's natural daughters. He later became Mayor of Bath.

It was in July 1724 that General Wade was ordered by George I 'to go in to the Highlands of Scotland, and narrowly to inspect the present situation of the Highlanders, their customs, manners and the state of the country, in regard to the depredations said to be committed in that part of your Majesty's dominions.' The allegations of 'depredations' had come from Lord Lovat, who had described in some detail the lawlessness, plunder, robbery and blackmail to which the clans were given. Reporting back in December 1724, Wade said that of the estimated 22,000 men capable of bearing arms in the Highlands and Islands, slightly more than half were 'ready to create new troubles, and rise in arms to favour the Pretender'. To the west of the Spey, Tummel and Tay, from Ross-shire to the Argyll coast, was a lawless land where the clans plundered their neighbours, lay in wait to rob the infrequent travellers, and ran a variety of protection rackets. One of the government's measures to prevent a recurrence of the Fifteen had been a scheme to disarm the Highlanders, with bounties for arms handed in and heavy punishment for those who held on to their weapons. But the Disarming Act had been a failure, Wade reported. The arms given up were old, useless pieces, good weapons being held back and concealed. Broken and useless arms had even been imported from Holland to be handed over against the bounty. Meanwhile, the Spaniards had re-armed some clans with new weapons.

Then Wade came to the point of most interest to readers of this book. He wrote:

I presume to observe to your Majesty the great disadvantage which regular troops are under when they engage with those who inhabit mountainous situations ... from want of Roads and Bridges, and from the excessive rains that almost continually fall in those parts; which, by nature and constant use, become habitual to the Natives, but very difficultly supported by the regular troops. They are unacquainted with the passages by which the mountains are traversed; exposed to frequent ambuscades, and shot from the tops of the hills, which they return without effect.

The situation Wade described, that of an undeclared guerrilla war, is sadly familiar in our own century, but 250 years ago it was fairly novel. In those days, wars were expected to be fought between the armies of recognized powers, normally without the intervention of, or much effect upon, the civil population. The military might be called in to quell a riot, as a policing operation, but it did not expect to find itself engaged in a running fight with civilians. Wade did not, as his equivalent or a civil service counterpart would have done today, inquire into the underlying causes of the Highland problem. Indeed, in an anonymous manuscript which passed into the hands of the Gartmore family, and subsequently into those of Sir Walter Scott, there is an implied criticism of Wade on this point. 'It is exceedingly strange,' the surprisingly liberal-minded report says, 'that the rebellion in the year 1715 did not awaken those in the administration to make their own steps towards civilising the

Highlands, for their own future security. The unhappy state of that country from the 1715, till the 1745, was the consequence of that neglect; and the unhappy state of the country was productive of those troubles in 1745.' The main problem, the document went on, was

there is not business for more than one half the number of people. ... The other half, then, must be idle, and beggars. ... That is, there are in the Highlands no fewer than 115,000 poor people ... [who] live an idle sauntering life among their acquaintances and relations, and are supported by their bounty; others get a livelihood by blackmail contracts, by which they receive certain sums of money from people of substance in the country, to abstain from stealing their cattle; and the last class of them gain their expense by stealing, robbing, and committing depredations.

All this was written in 1747, the year after Culloden, but it echoes almost exactly the description of Highland life given twenty-three years earlier in Lord Lovat's memorandum. Wade's instinct, expressed in his report to the King, was for repression rather than understanding. The result, in 1745, was a rebellion which, with a more capable leader, would undoubtedly have succeeded and which, even with the crippling disadvantage of having Prince Charles Edward at its head, very nearly did so. The lesson of the 1747 document has still to be learned in most of the world, not excluding Britain.

What Wade saw, however, was not over 100,000 half-starved, ill-clothed people living in mean huts which would hardly have given adequate shelter in the most equable of climates. He saw an affront to law and order. His programme for dealing with it was comprehensive. The independent companies of Highland troops established under William III, but later disbanded as ineffective and corrupt, should be revived as a police force. Properly controlled and regulated, Wade said, these troops were ideal for the purpose. They were 'inured to the fatigue of travelling the mountains, lying on the hills, wore the same habit, and spoke the same language' as the natives. A century and more later, the native African regiments were founded on the same reasoning. But the troops needed bases. Since 1715 forts had been built at Kilcumein (Fort Augustus) and at Inversnaid on Loch Lomondside, and barracks at Bernera, facing the Isle of Skye, and Ruthven, near Kingussie. Wade was not greatly impressed with these. They were undermanned, he said, having companies of only thirty soldiers in each, and two of them, Bernera and Inversnaid, were in the wrong places. Nevertheless, they should be strengthened, and Fort Augustus should be resited and expanded to be capable of housing up to a thousand men in an emergency. Fort Augustus was 'the most centrical part of the Highlands', and with the existing Fort William and Fort George at Inverness formed a means of control extending from the west coast to the east. (Wade's faith in this central line was shown, in the Forty-Five, to have been misplaced. It looked sensible enough on the map, but it was too vulnerable to incursions from the subsidiary glens which the Highlanders knew better than the occupying troops.) Communication between Fort Augustus and Inverness along Loch Ness, and the policing of the neighbouring territory, should be maintained by an armed galley carrying up to eighty men. At Ruthven Barracks, a regiment of dragoons should be stationed to check the southward movement of Highlanders, and stables should be built for that purpose.

Strangely, although Wade referred to the absence of suitable roads and bridges in the passage quoted earlier, no specific proposals for road-building were included in his recommendations of December 1724. However, by the following year, in a report on his progress, Wade noted that 'parties of regular troops have been constantly employed in making the roads of communication between Kilcumein and Fort William'. From then on, the plan for the whole basic network seems to have developed rapidly, for by 1726 the programme was well under way.

The four roads, totalling about 250 miles in length, actually projected and executed by Wade, or at any rate during his period of command in Scotland, were: from Inverness along the south side of Loch Ness to Fort William, the first to be made; from Dunkeld over the Drumochter Pass to Inverness; from Crieff by Aberfeldy and Tummel Bridge to join the Dunkeld to Inverness road at Dalnacardoch; and from Dalwhinnie, north of Drumochter, to Fort Augustus over the Corrieyairack Pass. There was an additional spur road, not accounted for in Wade's annual reports but clearly established by 1745, linking Ruthven with the Corrieyairack road and avoiding a tedious diversion via Dalwhinnie.

Built at an average cost of about £90 a mile, entirely by military labour, these are the roads on which Wade's considerable reputation

Ruthven Barracks

has been based. Nineteenth-century travellers to Scotland who so much admired his achievement tended to marvel at the 'simple soldier' who had pulled off such remarkable feats of engineering, or at the talented engineer who just happened to be in the army. In fact, neither assessment was correct. As his military record shows, Wade was no 'simple soldier'. Nor had he any engineering or surveying background except such as might be acquired by an officer in the field. His roads and bridges, though his most enduring monument, were only part of his plan for the pacification – or, to be more accurate, the repression – of the Highlands. He was doing a soldier's job: obeying orders, identifying the enemy and putting him down. After he left Scotland he went on to be a Privy Councillor, Lieutenant General of the Ordnance and ultimately, in 1744, Field Marshal and Commander-in-Chief in England. It was the career of a dedicated professional soldier who could have had no particular reason or aptitude to choose to build roads across Scotland's moors and bogs other than that it turned out to be in his line of duty. Why, then, the veneration? Why has the name of a general who died over 200 years ago been perpetuated on our Ordnance Survey maps, to the eclipse of his successors? Is there any deeper reason than that Wade was good (as he undoubtedly was) at self-advertisement?

I think there is. There had been maps of Scotland before Wade's time, notably Green's (1689) and Moll's (1725). The first complete record of Wade's work was produced by Thomas Willday in 1745, a few weeks before Culloden. The difference between them is striking, and not only for the addition of the Wade roads. In the years of Wade's posting in Scotland, the art of map-making had grown up, and no doubt this was due in part to the military disciplines that had been brought to road-building. The principles of ordnance and of surveying are similar; if you can lay a field of fire across a given landscape then you can make a road across it. The link was officially recognized in 1791 when the Ordnance Survey was founded, and it is possible, without great difficulty, to see Wade as one of its founding spirits.

To say that Wade did for Scotland what the Romans did for England (as some Victorian writers claimed) is apt enough up to a point, though the comparison should not be taken too literally. In extent, Wade's scheme was not nearly as ambitious as the Romans', though he faced engineering challenges such as the Romans never met. He was not laying down the communications system of an empire, but providing a more temporary expedient. As can be observed in some of the more abandoned sections, where Wade's road has been superseded by a newer one and allowed to decay, the quality of the construction did not match that of the Romans – and if anyone should put the decay down to the Highland climate and terrain, it should be remembered that the best-known surviving example of original Roman road in Britain goes over Blackstone Edge in Yorkshire, by no means a sympathetic environment. Indeed, a later Commander-in-Chief in Scotland, General Mackay, was scathing about Wade's roads, which, he reported in 1785, had 'in many places been very ill-constructed'. But then General Mackay had not actually had to do the job.

When Thomas Telford, the great civil engineer, was appointed engineer to the first Commissioners for Highland Roads and Bridges in 1803, he was uncharitable enough to remark that Wade's roads, having been built 'with other views than promoting Commerce and Industry', were 'generally in such Directions, and so inconveniently steep, as to be nearly unfit for the Purposes of Civil Life'. He was, of course, right in his assessment of Wade's motives; but it was uncharitable because Telford later made use of many of Wade's lines – and in particular the route over Drumochter – in composing his own system. The fact is that Wade often discovered the best, and sometimes the only, way through the Highlands' daunting terrain.

There are factors to be set against the criticisms of Wade's work. He was necessarily in a hurry, with only a limited time – twenty years, as it turned out – to complete the skeleton of a communications system. He used unskilled labour, supervised by lay officers. And he was building a system for use in a campaign. He doubtless would never have suggested that his roads had a commercial purpose, and in any case a commercial network already existed in the drove roads, which served the only commerce in the Highlands recognizable as such.

It is not clear how closely Wade was involved in the planning, design or building of the roads that were to take his name; though, in the manner of the day, he was ready enough to take the credit, whether this was in the form of a bilingual (Latin and English) inscription on the Tay Bridge at Aberfeldy or one of the many odes to him and his work scribbled by contemporary versifiers. He

certainly inspected the roads frequently, often spending the night in one of the 'huts' provided for official travellers. But his interest seems to have waned in the later years. After the arrival of Major William Caulfield in 1732 as Inspector of Roads, Wade seems to have left much of the work to him, and in 1734 and 1736 hardly visited Scotland at all.

Caulfield, like Wade an Irishman, was a professional military road-builder, perhaps the first of his kind in modern times. His experience began as a subaltern in charge of working parties on the Fort Augustus to Fort William road. He remained Inspector of Roads from 1732 until his death in 1767, and so covered the period in which the original four roads were developed or extended in several important directions. He was so much an admirer of Wade that he named his eldest son after him. Caulfield lived at Cradle Hall, near Inverness. He was evidently a good host, and Cradle Hall is said to have been named after a device like a modern builder's cradle by which his well-filled guests could be raised to their rooms after dinner. Caulfield is also said to have been the author of the lines:

> Had you seen these roads before they were made
> You would lift up your hands and bless General Wade,

and certainly the first line is Irish enough to make the story credible. There is, however, a slight mystery about this oft-quoted couplet.

An account of 1818 says that they were inscribed on a stone beside a road near Fort William, though the exact location is not given. But this seems to be the only reference to the wayside stone, whose inscription has been faithfully copied (though sometimes slightly altered) by later writers.

Much of what we know of methods of construction on the Wade roads and of the condition of the Highlands at the time comes from the writing of a mysterious and shadowy figure, Edward Burt. Some writers have described Burt as Wade's 'chief surveyor', but this accreditation seems to rest on an ambiguous sentence in his obituary in the *Scots Magazine*. He is also described in the same article as Wade's 'late agent', and this seems likely to be more accurate. Burton, the major Scottish historian, called Burt 'the clever engineer officer who assisted in the construction of Wade's roads', but Burt himself nowhere suggested that he was a serving soldier. According to one authority, 'Burt's real employment was to collect the rents of an unsold residue of the estates which had been forfeited after the rebellion of 1715'. This kind of job would go well with that of an agent for construction works, and probably Burt was a minor official who 'did a bit of this and that' as occasion allowed. There would be many such occasions: suppliers of provisions to be found and negotiated with, estate owners to be put in the picture about Wade's plans, horses and carts to be bought or hired. Burt's main interest so far as we are concerned here is that in Wade's period he was travelling extensively in the Highlands and wrote a series of letters which in 1754, a year before his death, were published as *Letters from a Gentleman in the North of Scotland*.

According to the *Letters*, Burt had a bad time in Scotland. The vile natives submitted him to humiliations, indignities and obscenities which he related at length. Offered disgusting stews that he could not bring himself to touch, he dined off dry bread. The curtains of his bed were 'fouled by dirty wenches'. He narrowly escaped being showered with filth from upstairs windows – a common risk in Edinburgh at that time but an unpleasant novelty to one so genteel. He was the first of a long line of travellers in Scotland to complain at the surly reception, poor food and shabby accommodation afforded by the inns. He was repelled by the squalor, cupidity and idleness of the Scots. Once, pressed to pardon a thief, he was told that 'the man's wife was one of the prettiest young women in the Highlands, and if I would pardon the husband I should have her.' He replied priggishly that it 'was an agreeable bribe, yet it could not prevail over the reasons I had to refer the affair to justice.' Nor were the Scots much impressed with Burt. Once, when he pompously declared that he represented the King, he received the retort: 'Hoot, mon! You represent His Majesty? He, God bless him, is muckle better represented on a bawbee!'

Notwithstanding all this, and the peevish and puffed-up tone of the *Letters*, the book ran into several editions, including one with an introduction by Sir Walter Scott, and became widely enough known to be the source of several long-standing myths about Scotland, including the one about the supposedly extraordinary purity of English as spoken in Inverness. The *Letters* were plundered extensively (though less widely acknowledged) by nineteenth-century writers on Scotland, including Macaulay, and are thus the source of what have now become off-the-peg judgements on the Highlands and their people. When, reading about the Highlanders of the eighteenth century and later, one finds words like 'wild' and 'savage' leaping from the page, one is unconsciously hearing the voice of Edward Burt.

The task that Wade set himself, as observed by Burt, was formidable. There were, in effect, no roads in the Highlands before 1725. The Highlanders used cattle paths for such shorter journeys as they made, and drove roads for more serious travelling. It was not in their interests to have well-defined tracks leading from one territory to another, and as they either went barefoot or wore thin brogues of untanned hide they had no wish for metalled surfaces. Highlanders, wrote one commentator, had 'a strong aversion to roads. The more inaccessible, the more secure, was their maxim.' The consequent isolation of the townships may be imagined, biting deeply into the spirit of the people. In 1733, Inverness Town Council sent a deputation to Dingwall, all of twenty miles away by road and less by ferry, to ascertain and report what sort of a place it was. Travellers and mail usually went to Scotland by sea, making their way inland only with difficulty and trepidation. As late as 1874, even after the opening of the Highland Railway, mail for the Spey valley went by sea to Inverness and then by foot messenger to Grantown.

'The old ways (for roads I shall not call them),' wrote Edward Burt, 'consisted chiefly of stony moors, bogs, rugged, rapid fords, declivities of hills, entangling woods and giddy precipices. 'You will say that this is a dreadful catalogue to be read to him that is about to take a Highland journey.' And so it was. The moors were strewn with boulders which Wade's soldiers had either to lever out of the way or undermine and sink. The bogs were fed with timber and faggots until a causeway was formed, but the cure was often only temporary. Fords cleared and made good would be in ruins after a season's floods, and Wade's early timber bridges (and some of his later stone ones) were no match for the weight of water that had to pass through them. Terrain and climate were so hostile that, later in the century after Wade's time, the expense of constant maintenance was found to be too great a burden on the public purse, and this was one reason – others were the relative peace of Scotland and the increasing threat of France – why the military roads were allowed to decay, a process which did not take long.

The standard width of a Wade road was sixteen feet, though it could narrow to as little as ten if the need arose. Whenever possible the roads ran straight, though they would take the easy route if there was a choice, even if this meant a deviation. The road-building season ran from May to October, when up to 500 men in parties of about 100 would be at work. Each detachment was commanded by a subaltern, with sergeants and corporals acting as foremen. Payment, on top of their soldiers' pay, was on a daily basis, but was made only for days on which work was actually done so that storms brought enforced and unpaid idleness. The subalterns received two shillings and sixpence ($12\frac{1}{2}$p) a day, sergeants one shilling (5p), corporals and drummers eightpence (about $3\frac{1}{2}$p) and ordinary soldiers sixpence ($2\frac{1}{2}$p).

For no one was life in the army in the eighteenth century easy, but few can have had it harder than these unskilled soldier–road-makers, ill equipped, ill shod and ill suited to their work. The eighteenth century saw no romance in moors and mountains; that was left for the affluent travellers of the next century to discover. The terrain was simply vast, difficult and awesome. The men were working in a hostile land, with only tented shelter, and on a diet consisting largely of biscuit, meal and cheese. Simple jacks and levers, spades, picks and shovels were their only tools, with gunpowder where necessary. When they did not meet open hostility from the natives, there was derision or superstition – sometimes both together. Burt tells of a 'very old wrinkled Highland woman' who stood watching a party of soldiers trying to remove a boulder from their path. 'What are the fools a-doing?' she cried in Gaelic. 'That stone will lie there for ever, for all them.' Burt goes on: 'But when she saw that vast bulk begin to rise, she set up a hideous Irish yell, took to her heels, ran up the side of a hill just by, like a young girl, and never looked behind her while she was within our sight. I make no doubt she thought it was magic, and the workmen warlocks.'

Perhaps not surprisingly, the soldiers sought refuge from the weather, the natives and the fatigue in drink, when they could. To help control this problem it was ruled that only subsistence money should be paid to working parties until the end of their tours of duty, and that no credit should be asked from, or given by, the suttlers, provision traders, who accompanied the working parties. It was not a case of not asking for credit because a refusal might offend; for asker and giver alike, giving credit was a court-martial matter, soldiers and civilians both being subject to military law.

Well-meaning travellers could undo the effects of these regulations. Travelling along the road from Fort Augustus to Bernera after Wade's time, on their journey to the Western Isles, Johnson and Boswell met up with a party of soldier–road-builders and gave them two shillings to drink. Putting up for the night at Anoch (now Ceannacroc), the travellers were joined by the soldiers who, according to Johnson, 'had the true military impatience of coin in their pockets, and had marched at least six miles to find the first place where liquor could be bought.' Johnson gave them another shilling each, which 'detained them in the barn, either merry or quarrelling, the whole night, and in the morning they went back to their work with great indignation at the bad qualities of whisky.'

If whisky or the Highlanders were not troubling the soldiers, there were always the midges. The Highland midge, *Culicoides impunctatus*, is notorious. In the late 1940s it was considered enough of a menace to justify *two* government reports, and the ecologist Fraser Darling has written that 'a greatly increased tourist industry to the West Highlands could be encouraged if the midge could be controlled.' Burt, too, had something to say about the problem: 'These [midges] are so very small that, separately, they are but just perceptible and that is all; and, being of a blackish colour, when a

Near Fort Augustus

number of them settle upon the skin, they make it look as if it was dirty; there they soon bore with their little augers into the pores, and change the face from black to red.' Walkers should be warned that the midges are still there, though modern creams are fairly effective.

It has already been indicated that Wade, Caulfield and the rest got no thanks for their efforts from the lowly people of the Highlands (and indeed there was no reason why they should). Nor were the chiefs and lairds – even those disposed to the King's cause – any more enthusiastic. They complained that the new roads, while the Highlanders did not wish to use them themselves, opened up the country to strangers, with consequent prejudice to security. (Similar fears were expressed over 150 years later, when the West Highland Railway was being planned.) Bridges would 'render the ordinary people effeminate, and less fit to pass the waters in other places where there are none'. There was the expense of shoeing horses if the roads were to be used – Highland horses were unshod. These objections might have been overcome if Wade's roads had led to markets or fisheries, but so far from serving the purposes of the lairds Wade often did the reverse, as on the Atholl estate – taking over estate roads to build into his own. But Thomas Pennant, who travelled in the Highlands in 1769, suspected the landowners of baser motives. 'By admitting strangers among them,' he wrote, 'their clans were taught that the lairds were not the first of men.' As for the peasants, according to Pennant, 'as long as they had their waters, their torrents and their bogs in a state of nature, they made their excursions, could plunder and retreat with their booty in full security.'

Wade and his English contemporaries were, however, well satisfied with the work. Wade caused to be inscribed on the Tay Bridge at Aberfeldy a laudatory tablet referring to his own skill in carrying out 'this arduous undertaking'. Burt described the new roads as being 'as smooth as Constitutional Hill', causing a twentieth-century writer, Dr A. R. B. Haldane, to comment tartly that 'it is difficult to avoid the conclusion that this was either a gross overstatement or a sad commentary on the state of the streets of contemporary London.' Thomas Pennant, no mean hyperbolist, described Wade as 'another Hannibal'. And Wade himself, reporting to the Prime Minister, Walpole, in 1731, found himself able to say of the newly completed road over the Corrieyairack Pass that it was 'now made as easy and practicable for wheel carriage as any road in the country'. (He was, however, about the only person with a good word to say for this particular road, then or since, except for modern walkers who enjoy it for its very ruggedness and challenge.)

And then there were the poets.

> When ages hence, his last line's lengthener dies
> And his lost dust reveals not where it lies,
> Still shall his living greatness guard his name
> And his works lift him to immortal fame,

wrote one, an anonymous Scottish clergyman, of General Wade in the course of a long and wearying encomium. And when the first known published version of 'God Save the King' appeared in the *Gentleman's Magazine* in October 1745 it included the following verse:

> God grant that Marshal Wade
> May by Thy mighty aid
> Victory bring.
> May he sedition hush
> And like a torrent rush
> Rebellious Scots to crush –
> God save the King!

Wade was at this time in command of the English forces, a post he was not to hold for much longer.

But Wade's successors, both civil and military, were critical of him as a road-builder. Thomas Telford and General Mackay have already been quoted. Mackay was hard on the bridges as well as the roads. 'Many of them,' he reported, 'are insufficient, some ruinous, and others of those that were first built, injudiciously constructed and ill-executed.' And it was true that a distressing number of the early Wade bridges fell down, too little account having been taken of the might of Scottish waters in flood. A nineteenth-century Chief Inspector of Roads in the Highlands, Joseph Mitchell, also criticized Wade's building techniques as encouraging the formation of snow-drifts. Wade seems to have taken little notice of underlying strata, and to have been of the 'bash on regardless' school of thought – though, to be fair, perhaps that was all he could do with the labour skills at his disposal. On moorland stretches, his men scraped away until rock or gravel appeared, making a bank on either side, and then laid a top dressing. This consisted of layers of stones gradually decreasing in size, followed (according to Burt, who must surely have been exaggerating) by 'two, three or four more feet of gravel, to fill up the interstices of the smaller stones and form a smooth and binding surface'. Some account was taken of the need for drainage, though this seems to have been fairly primitive and vulnerable to the winter's damage, so that surface repairs on the roads already built were the first priority of each new season's work. The effect of the ditch and bank formation, according to Mitchell, was simply to trap snow on the road – though it is fair to add that even today's technology can find nothing better to cope with this problem than lengths of chestnut snow fencing which, laid apparently haphazardly across adjacent slopes, looks more primitive than it probably is.

The sketching in of the military road system proceeded steadily after Wade's time until, at its peak about 1767, some thousand miles with almost as many bridges were said to be either completed or under construction. For just over forty years' work, using unskilled labour and the most basic of tools, this was – despite later criticism – not bad going. But from 1767 on, coinciding with the death of Caulfield, the standard of maintenance declined so that by 1790, when the employment of military labour ceased and repairs were

Ski slopes near Cock Bridge

contracted out to civilians, only about 600 miles remained in reasonable repair and many of these were fast reverting to nature.

Between Wade's departure from Scotland in 1737 and Caulfield's death thirty years later, roads were built from Stirling to Crieff and from Dumbarton to Inveraray, the latter (the 'Rest-and-be-thankful' road wrongly ascribed by Dorothy Wordsworth, as noted earlier, to Wade) taking over five years to complete owing to the difficulty of the route and the interruption of the Forty-Five. Attention then turned to linking Stirling and Fort William by way of Tyndrum, the Black Mount and the Devil's Staircase (part of which is treated in detail in a later chapter) and Blairgowrie and Fort George by way of Braemar (which includes the Lecht Road, also walked for this book). The system at its peak was completed with a road from Inveraray by way of Dalmally to join the Fort William road at Tyndrum (substantially along the same lines as today's road), and one from Tarbet to Crianlarich, providing a short cut between Dumbarton and Fort William. Away from the West Highlands proper, a road was built about 1760 from Contin, near Dingwall, to Poolewe on the west coast, then the main port for the Isle of Lewis. It must have followed the line of the present A832 through Achnasheen, but it seems to have been maintained for only about twenty years before being allowed to decline.

Meanwhile Wade's life had ended in shade, if not in shadow. By 1745 he was seventy-two years of age, and should clearly not have been expected to play a commanding role in putting down the new rebellion. But he took to the field like the old warhorse that he was. It was a mistake. His thinking had slowed, and twice – first on the Highlanders' way south after Prestonpans, and again on their march north from Derby – he was outmanouevred by an enemy with no great campaigning skills. Getting the message, he retired from his post and went back to the quiet and grace of Bath, where he died in 1748. Unlike Cope, who had to stand court martial for his equally poor performance in the Forty-Five, Wade escaped with his reputation – in public, at least – undiminished, and although it is said that in his latter days in command he was known as 'Grandmother Wade' a still grateful nation buried him in Westminster Abbey. He had never married, but left behind four natural children; and 250 miles of Scottish roads.

3
Over the Corrieyairack

The twenty-eight miles between Dalwhinnie and Fort Augustus over the Corrieyairack Pass include the longest single stretch of Wade road left more or less as it was built; that is, as far as the route is concerned, for there has been some recent attention to the actual surface in many places. The heart of the road, for walkers, is the twelve miles or so between Melgarve in the south and Cullachy House on the outskirts of Fort Augustus – a rough track which goes over the summit of the pass at over 2500 feet and affords a truly panoramic view of the Highlands. The pass itself is one of Scotland's great watersheds; to the north, the streams feed Loch Ness, to the south the Spey. To cross it, you commit yourself to a demanding walk over very exposed and often inhospitable country. For miles on end there is no kind of shelter. The country each side of the pass usually has weather of its own, so walkers should be prepared for any eventuality. It is not a walk to be rushed, and a degree of planning is needed unless you are camping overnight.

This introduction is not written lightly. The Corrieyairack road has had a reputation for savage conditions ever since it was built. An account of a journey over it in the 1790s describes the road as 'rough, dangerous and dreadful', and the traveller, who was on horseback, 'thought it almost a miracle to escape unhurt from such horrid wastes, roaring torrents, unwholesome vapour and frightful fogs; drenched from top to toe, frozen with cold, and half-dead with fatigue.' There are other stories of carriages blown over precipices by the wind, soldiers lost in the snow and wandering mindlessly off onto the moor, and travellers struck down from exposure on the road itself. In 1804 the Corrieyairack road was, according to the lairds of Inverness-shire, 'from its height at all times dangerous, and generally impassable for four months in the year, to the prejudice of his Majesty's service, and the loss of the lives of many of his soldiers and subjects.' The central and most hazardous section, from Melgarve to Cullachy House, is no more populated – indeed, is probably less

The road from Dalwhinnie

so – than it was at the beginning of the nineteenth century, and so once you set out you can expect to be on your own until you reach the other end. Yet this is, of course, the major attraction of the walk; there are not many places accessible to the ordinary non-hearty walker where you can get an agreeable sense of adventure and a pleasant degree of challenge provided you take sensible basic care. The warning here is only meant to discourage you from setting out, as I once met a family of four doing from Melgarve, dressed only in jeans, tee-shirts and training shoes. This was in August, but I had already that day felt sick with cold at the summit.

The complete road ran from Dalwhinnie, where it branched off the Dunkeld to Inverness route, to a point on the Inverness to Fort William road near Cullachy House outside Fort Augustus. Its strategic importance was fundamental to Wade's scheme for the control of the Highlands. He needed an alternative route north in case his main 'Highland Road' through Strathspey was cut; and he needed to be able to strike at the heart of the lands of the disaffected clans in and around the Great Glen without travelling ponderously and circuitously by way of Inverness. The configuration the Highlands present between the Spey and the Great Glen is a series of great shelves running from southwest to northeast. It was no mean feat to find a way across so that Fort Augustus, the centre point of Wade's command of the Great Glen, could be served from both Edinburgh and Stirling. However it was done, it was bound to be difficult, and certainly no other Wade road presented such an unremitting challenge to the men who built it or the troops who were to travel along it. It may be significant that the only successful use to which the Corrieyairack road was put was, as we shall see in this chapter, by soldiers reasonably familiar with the territory – and in August at that.

It is interesting to speculate on Wade's reasons for choosing Dalwhinnie for the junction of the Corrieyairack road. Other than that it was an overnight stop for drovers, the decision seems to have been fairly arbitrary, and it seems also that Wade later recognized his mistake. The most substantial fortification in this area was Ruthven Barracks near Kingussie, but to reach it from the Corrieyairack involved, initially, either a time-consuming diversion southwards to Dalwhinnie and then north along the Inverness road or a wearying slog along cattle paths to cut off the corner. The mistake was eventually rectified (though, curiously, Wade's records and reports are silent as to dates) by the building of a spur road from Laggan through Catlodge to Crubenbeg (described in Chapter 5), which was in use in time for the early stages of the Forty-Five. But Wade's system would have been more logical and more secure if the spur road had been his primary route and the junction had been established from the first at Crubenbeg.

It is possible to trace on the map (and, at least partially, on the ground, if you have a fair amount of time, a good deal of determination, and avoid the shooting season) an alternative route by which Wade, starting from Ruthven, might have reached Fort Augustus. Unless you are full of pioneering spirit, it is best done in two stages. From the Ruthven end, the putative route begins rather unpromisingly (though things rapidly improve) at the turning opposite the village hall in Newtonmore, which would have been reached from Ruthven by way of the ferry across the Spey just northeast of

Kingussie (Chapter 5). After a steepish climb out of Newtonmore, you quickly emerge on to a plateau with splendid views (and, I'm told, spectacularly photogenic cloud effects towards sunset). The public road continues as far as Shepherd's Bridge over the River Calder, after which a track follows the east side of Allt Fionndrigh for about three miles before petering out. Here, Wade's troubles would have begun, but if he had headed up Glean Ballach under the crags of Càrn Dearg, and then turned westward, it would have been no more of a challenge than the summit of the Corrieyairack and could have been surmounted by traverses in a similar manner. Once across the watershed somewhere near Beinn Odhar, he would have passed south of Meàllan Odhar and followed the line taken by a track leading down to Sronlairig Lodge. This part of the route can be walked from the Whitebridge end, some nine miles away, making a pleasant and dryshod day out.

However, Wade did not choose this route, and probably did not even consider it. For one thing, he did not have the benefit of

Between Newtonmore and Laggan

modern Ordnance Survey maps; for another, he *did* have the benefit of an existing route over the Corrieyairack, shown as a road on a map of 1725 but probably, in truth, only a drove road. Certainly, for some 200 years the Corrieyairack was one of the major channels for black cattle and, later, sheep, driven from the islands and western Highlands to the markets in the south, and there are accounts of stock passing this way until the last years of the nineteenth century. It is not difficult to trace the end of the Corrieyairack as a drove road: the West Highland Railway reached Fort William in 1894, and Mallaig in 1901, and a branch line from Spean Bridge to Fort Augustus was opened in 1903.

Wade started work on the Corrieyairack road, the last of the four built under his command, in 1731 and virtually completed it in the same year. Four working parties began in April and two more joined in in July. On 30 October, all six working parties – over 500 men – were able to gather at the Allt Lagan a' Bhainne, on the northern side of the pass, for a triple celebration of the King's birthday, the completion of the road, and the end of the road-building season, and no doubt the last of these gave the greatest pleasure. For each of the working parties there was an ox roasted whole, liquor was on hand in abundance and, says a contemporary report, 'the joy was great'. Wade was evidently not present, having already left Scotland for the south as was his habit as winter came on, but that autumn he felt able to report to the government that the Corrieyairack road, 'made through a part of the country that was scarcely passable for man or horse', was 'now made as easy and practicable for wheel carriage as any road in the country'. The total cost, he noted, was just under £3300, and the fact that he was still owed the odd £300 may have accounted for his slight exaggeration of the 'then and now'. Of the many contemporary descriptions of the Corrieyairack road, none except Wade's suggest that, even when new, it was anything but perilous. When, in the early nineteenth century, Thomas Telford was engaged to construct Scotland's first civil road system, he averted his eyes from the Corrieyairack Pass and chose instead to reach the Great Glen by the Laggan road from Drumgask to Spean Bridge. (It was a wise engineering decision, but the Laggan road ran into financial and other difficulties, including the bankruptcy of the contractor responsible for half of it, and finally took thirteen years to complete.)

Laggan from the west

The first ten miles of the Corrieyairack road, from Dalwhinnie, make fairly dull walking across bleak and heavily fenced moorland along the A889, which is busy in summer. The road leads off to the left from the AA box on the north side of the railway bridge north of Dalwhinnie, though the railway has obliterated the original junction here. Unless your taste in accommodation is eccentric, you will not want to use Dalwhinnie as a base; I suggest that you take the first ten miles of the road as walked (in truth, you will miss little) and set up base in Laggan or Drumgask, where there is hotel and self-catering accommodation in more agreeable surroundings.

If you take a car to Melgarve, where the tarred road ends, the walk to the summit of the pass and back takes most of a good summer day, and later you can leave the car at Fort Augustus and walk to the summit and back from the north – another good day's work. If you want to tackle the whole walk in one direction, you'll need to book a night's stay ahead, and it's easier to do this at Fort Augustus than in the smaller settlements at the southern end. It is a great pity, as has often been remarked, that the former kingshouse at

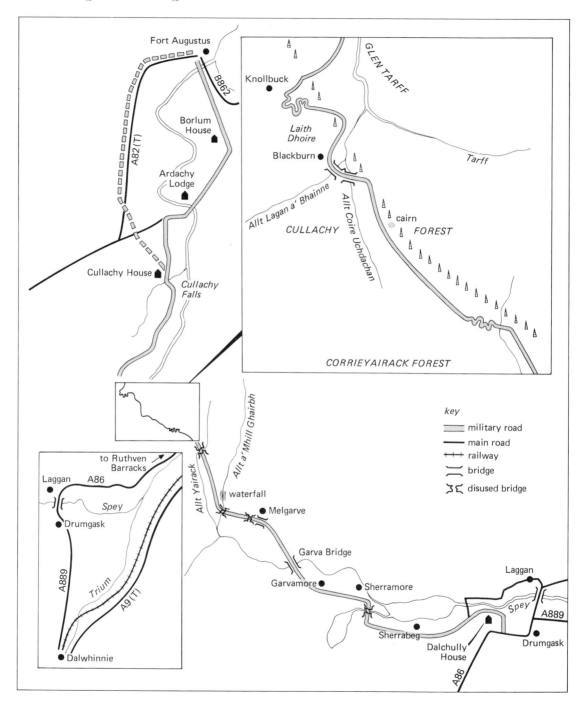

Garvamore was not kept going as an inn or youth hostel, since it would have made forward planning unnecessary, but it must have fallen on hard times after droving finished; and even today, when Scotland can sometimes seem fairly swarming with walkers in summer, few of them seem to pass this way. As far as difficulty goes, there's not much to choose between the southward and northward journeys; the stiff climb up the zigzags from the south is fairly evenly matched by a long haul above Glen Tarff if you are coming from Fort Augustus.

The way to Melgarve today is over the metal bridge at Laggan, turning very sharp left on the north side to double back through the village, but Wade kept to the south side of the Spey as far as Garva Bridge. His line can be seen falling away to the right of the Spean Bridge road, the A86, about a mile west of Drumgask. It joins the drive to Dalchully House and then turns left along the south bank of the river. After about a mile, the new road recrosses the Spey to meet the old, and the two become one from this point on. Between Sherrabeg and Sherramore, land drainage works take the new road off the Wade line for a few hundred yards, but his track can be followed across a now isolated and redundant bridge. From here on, the Spey valley becomes increasingly neat, well tended and lush. Drovers and their beasts must have welcomed these pleasant pastures after their long drive over the pass, and this was a convenient stopping place before the next leg of their journey, to Dalwhinnie.

It was hereabouts that an order was given which may well have changed the course of English and Scottish history. What is certain is that if, in the opening stages of the Forty-Five, the Hanoverian army under Cope had met Prince Charles Edward's army in the pass, Corrieyairack would have been added to the list of bloody battles between English and Scots, and the English would have been massacred. What might have followed such an ignominious defeat for the English so early in the rebellion can scarcely be imagined.

Since Prince Charles Edward, Bonnie Prince Charlie, the Young Pretender, is about to make his first appearance of several in the course of these walks, this is perhaps the moment to declare a view of him. The romantic figure of legend, created initially by himself, perpetuated by Scott and a myriad of lesser writers and carried on into our own time by such manifestations as the film starring David Niven, does not stand up too well when confronted with the facts.

Laggan Bridge and Drumgask

Most of us would like to believe in all the Bonnie Prince Charlie apparatus – the Skye Boat Song, 'Will ye no' come back again?', the king over the water, and all the rest of it – if only because so many people, including the Prince himself, have worked so long and hard at it. But for all that he was given to such princely pretensions as making entrances on a white horse, touching sufferers from the king's evil and bending a gracious ear to the flatteries of the ladies of Edinburgh, contemporary portraits of him (whose painters would have been doing the best they could with the material at their disposal) show a conceited, slightly pettish figure, features which were to settle, as later portraits show, into a permanent expression of surly resentment. His relationship with the clans that followed him was one of using and being used, like that of most rebel leaders throughout history, and the heroic aura he had built round himself was smashed to pieces when he delivered himself, after Culloden, of his infamous exit line, 'Let every man seek his own safety as best he can.' With friends in high French places, it was all very well for him, but 120 of his followers were hunted down and killed, and another 700 or so simply disappeared. Safe on the Continent, Charles lived on until 1788, still pretending, but with his romantic image slipping gradually into drink, enlivened with bouts of wife- and mistress-bashing. Margaret Forster, in her biography *The Rash Adventurer* (Secker and Warburg, 1973), has delivered a precise and cutting comment: 'Only ladies in Highland Industry shops speak of him with any affection, which seems appropriate since all Charles bequeathed to Scotland that was of any benefit was a tourist industry.'

In 1745, however, things looked very different for Prince Charles, and it was the building of the Corrieyairack road that enabled him to make his challenging march south to open his campaign. He had raised his standard, in front of a force of 1300 men quickly inflated by rumour to 3000, at Glenfinnan on the Fort William to Arisaig road on 19 August. He had been canvassing support among the clans for almost a month, but not all who had promised came forward. (This was Cope's experience also, suggesting that, as so often in colonialist wars, the natives were refusing to let their hearts and minds be won by either side but were holding back until it became clearer which way the wind blew.) The raising of the standard, together with the proclamation of Prince Charles as regent and the reading of his manifesto, was to have been a heroic occasion, but in the event it was rather lacking in splendour. The proclamation and various other 'state' papers were read out by the former Duke of Atholl, who had forfeited his estates after 1715. He was an old man now, and had to be supported by two assistants because of his gout. The manifesto was long and, by all accounts, tedious. This was not what the clansmen had joined Prince Charles for, and they began to get restless. It was, in truth, a ramshackle army, clothed and armed with what its soldiers had been able to find, steal or borrow. Wade's fears in 1724 of the number and quality of weapons concealed by the disaffected Highlanders do not seem to have been borne out. Little thought appears to have been given as to how the Highlanders would be fed and housed on their long march, now that friendly natives were no longer assured. It was, however, a large enough force to frighten the enemy, and when the news from Glenfinnan reached General Sir John Cope in Stirling it galvanized him into action.

History has not been kind to Cope, who was, as Scotland's historian Burton says, 'destined by his ludicrous failure in an emergency to a wide but unenvied notoriety'. If Prince Charles's army was a ragtag and bobtail lot, Cope's was not much better. Few of his infantry, and none of his cavalry, had seen action. The force Cope scraped together for his march to meet the Prince consisted of some 1400 men. 'To penetrate with such a force a mountain district inhabited by a large body of hostile armed men,' Burton wrote, 'seemed a project bordering on insanity; but the vain expectation was entertained that the well-affected clans would flock to his standard.' Cope's object was then to nip the rebellion in the bud before the Prince was able to move south and pick up more support on the way. Pressed by his superiors to get on with it, Cope left Stirling on 20 August, well stocked with supplies including a drove of black cattle and a cache of 1000 weapons for distribution among the well-affected clansmen; but without, as yet, a clear idea of where the march would end. Though weak in most things, the Prince was strong on counter-intelligence. He had been fortunate enough to capture a handful of Hanoverian garrison officers. These he released at intervals 'on parole', knowing that they would make their way to Cope and report what they had seen and heard. He could thus arrange for Cope to receive a trickle of information calculated to keep him on edge and uncertain of the Jacobite army's intentions. But the first piece of bad news Cope received, at Crieff, was from his own side. The young Duke of Atholl and Lord Glenorchy, both of whom had promised support, had been unable to persuade their tenants likewise.

Things got worse for Cope. The bread went mouldy. The baggage horses broke away from the train. There were numerous desertions. The army toiled on to Dalnacardoch, which they reached after five days. Here, they were met by Captain Sweetenham, who had been captured by the Jacobites, had witnessed the celebrations at Glenfinnan, and was then released as a 'plant'. Sweetenham duly reported that the Prince had 3000 men on the march and was planning to confront Cope in the upland wastes of the Corrieyairack Pass.

It seems obvious today that even if Cope had been given correct information on the strength of the Prince's army, it would have been suicidal to throw an inexperienced force, trained (in so far as it was trained in anything) in textbook warfare, into conflict with an army of native soldiers who knew the terrain, had the commanding height

Laggan

of the pass and had, at that stage, morale overwhelmingly on their side. While he considered the options, Cope marched on, reaching Dalwhinnie on 26 August and taking the Corrieyairack road the next day. It is not clear whether his mind had been made up at this stage to avoid a confrontation and instead lead his army to Inverness; it has been suggested that from Dalwhinnie onwards the march towards the Corrieyairack was a feint. However that may have been, it afterwards looked like indecision – or worse. The army's vanguard reached a point near Sherramore and then turned back the way it had come, taking the spur road from Catlodge to Ruthven. Cope's decision that day featured among the many charges brought against him at his court martial (presided over by Wade) in 1746. He was acquitted on all counts ('his attacking the rebels, on the Corrie-yairack, with any prospect of success, was impracticable,' said the findings), but his historical reputation suffered all the same.

Meanwhile, on 27 August, Prince Charles had formulated his plan to ambush Cope in the pass. He had brought from France some twenty field guns, which he planned to dispose at the head of the pass. When these had done their worst, his men would sweep down on Cope's survivors as they laboured up the eighteen steep traverses from the south. But when the advance detachment of the Jacobites reached the summit, expecting to see Cope's vanguard moving up the long slope beside the Allt Yairack from Melgarve, they found the valley still. Burton reports: 'It is said that the Highlanders uttered shouts of exultation when they learned the evasion of Cope. Yet it was the escape of an enemy certain, if he ascended the hill, to fall into their hands.' There is nothing like an easy victory – especially one gained without a shot being fired – to raise the spirits, and the Jacobites pressed on down the Corrieyairack in fine style, thus contributing the ironic footnote to Wade's work of fifteen years before that the first effective use of a Wade road was by an enemy army. Skirting Badenoch, they picked up Cluny Macpherson and his well-disciplined force of three hundred men. Poor Cluny; he had been undecided in his choice of leader, and seems to have followed the Prince almost on an impulse. The impulse was to lead, within a few months, to the beginning of seven years of self-imprisonment in a cave below Creag Dhubh, within sight of Ruthven.

Passing the spot where Cope's vanguard halted – one can imagine the scene: the officers conferring quietly, the troops grumbling and wondering, muscles being eased and ankles stretched as new orders

Near Garvamore

were awaited – the road to Corrieyairack leads past Garvamore to the splendid twin-arched and heavily buttressed Garva Bridge, 180 feet long. The tarred road continues as far as the new wooden bridge at Melgarve, and just short of this there is ample parking space if you have driven this far. Just beyond, beside a cottage, is a small bridge which has been broken through but is not yet in total ruin. Peering through the hole, one can see the construction of wedge-shaped rocks, roughly but carefully tapered. At the base of the northeast corner of this bridge is one of the few personal mementoes left by Wade's road-builders – the inscription *W B* or perhaps *W3* on one of the stones, rather carefully, though not professionally, cut with neat serifs to the *W*. This discovery led me to others, mostly imagined, in similar positions on other Wade bridges, and leads me now to the thought that it might not be a bad idea to pack heelball and paper with your oatcakes and maps. If there are marks to be found, they are likely to be more susceptible to rubbing than to photography. A few hundred yards further on, however, there is no doubt about the distinct triangulation mark on a commonplace-looking rock on the left-hand side of the track. When I saw it, the arrowhead was picked out in moss. Here, where the boulders dotting the roadside might well have been heaved out of the way by Wade's men while cackling Highland women looked on, you feel very close to the military road-builders.

Before the road turns half-right to meet the Allt Yairack – Wade was very economical with his alignments here – there is another broken Wade bridge, now repaired with a new wooden deck, and, on the north side, the remains of a substantial milehouse or guard post, now occupied by sheep. Above it to the right, the Allt a'Mhill Ghairbh rushes to meet the Yairack down a pleasant though modest waterfall, beside which is a dry and sheltered picnic spot – by no means common along this road. Turning now alongside the Yairack, the way ahead is clearly marked by the line of pylons. The building of the grid line from the north, through the pass, was the last commercial use made of the Corrieyairack road. Strangely enough, the pylons do not seem to intrude, and it is easy to see why the thirties poets like Day Lewis and Louis MacNeice saw them as optimistic symbols; though a less romantic eye must recognize that they are carrying power *away* from the Highlands where it is generated, often past abandoned cottages that could have breathed

Near Melgarve

new life if only they could have taken advantage of the power that passes them by. Pylons and road run together along the Yairack, crossing it in the floor of the valley beside the remains of what was once a bridge, on top of which, one August day, I found a fine crop of blueberries.

The blueberries were exceptional. This side of the pass is strangely thin in wild life. Heather grows sparsely. Birds and even insects are rare. Apart from a family of ptarmigan disturbed near the top of the zigzags I saw, on a relatively mild day, only a few moths and the occasional bee. Except when low-flying aircraft on training missions sweep across from Glen Roy to the Spey – a sobering reminder of how a Highland rebellion would be put down today – everything is abnormally quiet.

Now the long haul up the zigzags begins. You can see it coming well ahead, and it looks fairly impossible. In Wade's day there were eighteen legs, each buttressed on the lower side. Now there are only thirteen, and only odd traces of the buttresses remain. There is, however, a convenient baulk of timber to rest on at the fifth bend (and I, for one, needed it), and after the eleventh the way becomes straighter and less demanding. It needs a considerable effort to imagine an army with its baggage, limbers and other impedimenta scaling these bends, but there is an account of the scene passed on by the intrepid Scottish traveller, the Hon. Mrs Sarah Murray, in her 1799 *Companion and Useful Guide to the Beauties of Scotland*. She describes the crossing of the Corrieyairack from north to south in 1746 by a company of the 24th Regiment under one Major Barry:

The officers, to add to the uncommonness of the scene, ordered the men to walk one by one down the zigzag; and the baggage and women to bring up the rear on horseback. What an extraordinary appearance in such a desert! To see a military moving zigzag of almost two miles; their arms glittering in the summer sunbeams, shining full upon them, and their officers at the bottom admiring the sight!

It has to be said that the huts of the electricity board lend a certain tackiness to the summit, far removed from the Hon. Mrs Sarah Murray's romantic picture, and on the north side of the huts an apparently disused pylon, with no cables attached to it, might well be removed. The true summit is about half a mile beyond the electricity station, marked by a small cairn. Here, to the northwest, the whole of the Western Highlands are laid out before you, and beyond Fort Augustus the old military road to Bernera Barracks at Glenelg can be seen climbing through the forests of Glen Moriston with, far beyond, Kintail and the mountains of Wester Ross.

From the summit, it is a more gentle walk down and across the watershed. This side of the pass is altogether milder and, for the botanist or bird-watcher, more interesting. Soon, you move into an area of upland pasture, still supporting cattle and sheep and no doubt one of the attractions of the Corrieyairack road as a drover's way. Certainly there can have been nothing to support stock between here and the Speyside lands, and the road over the pass must have been a stretch that drovers and beasts alike tackled with their teeth gritted. The bridge over the Allt Coire Uchdachan is one of Wade's, rebuilt under the auspices of the Scottish Rights of Way Society in the 1920s, and the modern Bailey bridge, erected in 1961 by a squad of Royal Engineers, a little way north, crosses the Allt Lagan a' Bhainne and marks the spot where the feast to commemorate the completion of the road, mentioned earlier, was held. Past Blackburn and up a slope of open moorland, the descent to Cullachy begins, with another set of zigzags – punishing enough if you are approaching from the north, but not in the same class as those on the other side of the summit – taking the road down beside the River Tarff across the shoulder of Liath Dhoire. At the top of the zigzags is a small flat-topped area known as 'Prince Charlie's dining table' from the legend that he and his officers had a meal there on their way to meet Cope. There appears not to be an excess of authority for this story, but what is certain is that, commanding as it does a view in one direction of Fort Augustus and in the other of the summit of the pass, it would have made an ideal signal station. Another vantage point becomes visible as you descend the zigzags – the ruined but still very neat croft of Knollbuck on the hillside facing you. The track leads fairly steeply down to the valley of the Tarff, passing, a few yards off the track to the right, another waterfall which makes a pleasant rest stop. At the bottom the vegetation is so lush and varied as to be like a well-tended garden; one of the most notable inhabitants, beside the track and on the slope towards the stream, is the saxifrage grass-of-Parnassus, lending a cultivated air to the scene. The track takes a sharp right turn over the stream, and Wade's is the leftward of the two tracks ahead. From here, about a mile of easy walking takes you through a gate off the moor onto a metalled road passing by Cullachy House, and so down to the public road.

The route followed by Wade from here into Fort Augustus is said to have been roughly along the line of the present road past Cullachy House and Ardachy Lodge, turning left to Borlum House and so into the town from the west side of the Tarff. However, evidence for this is none too clear, and I am tempted to believe that the Wade road went across the present road, down a clearly defined but overgrown track towards the present A82, and then along a line which can be seen, in places, on the north side of the main road. There is, incidentally, a limited amount of parking space opposite the end of the Wade road, near Cullachy House, if you wish to walk the Corrieyairack from this end.

4

Crieff to Dalnacardoch

The road from Crieff to Dalnacardoch, the third in Wade's sequence, was built in 1730, though its centrepiece and, in Wade's eyes, his crowning achievement, the Tay Bridge at Aberfeldy, was not completed until three years later. Like the Corrieyairack road, it was based on a drover's way, and this trade was supporting inns and small settlements before Wade's time. After the road's military phase had passed, it was reconstructed in the 1820s by Thomas Telford, but it remained in droving use until the end of the nineteenth century. A long stretch north of Tummel Bridge still has the wide verges characteristic of droves. At Dalwhinnie, to the north, the stock driven across the Corrieyairack was joined by droving traffic from Sutherland by way of Muir of Ord, and this mass of beasts – at the height of the season, in late August and early September, more than 1000 head a day – was funnelled across Glen Errochty and by Tummel Bridge to the great markets at Crieff and Falkirk. The trade began as soon as practicable, in April, and continued until late November. Crieff marks the boundary between Highlands and Lowlands and, given the difficulties attendant upon all travel in those days, was equally accessible to drovers from the north and buyers from the south. From about 1700 to 1750 it was Scotland's premier cattle market, or tryst, seeing the sale of 30,000 head of black cattle in an average year. The market took place in mid-October, and, as might be expected with the sudden inrush of a rootless population, the good burghers of Crieff were greatly incensed by the temporary onset of lawlessness. It was reported that if drovers fancied a billet, they would take it by force, driving the lawful inhabitants out for the time being and, when they left, making away with any portable household goods. Perhaps it was this that led the Earl of Perth, who owned the market and the right to exact twopence for each beast, to set about 'improving' Crieff, creating a neat, planned town in the English style based on the hand-weaving of wool. It may be that the tryst moved on because it felt it was not wanted. At all events, the importance of Crieff declined from about 1750 onwards, giving way to Falkirk, though Crieff remained an important stopping place on the drove road. In turn, the railways, in the late nineteenth century, killed droving altogether, but by this time Falkirk had turned its attention to heavy industry and Crieff to the holiday trade. By the 1890s Crieff had skilfully adapted itself into a Scottish spa, equipped with four hotels, 'numerous lodgings and villas for summer', and a suitable range of shops. For the road to Dalnacardoch and the settlements along it there was a period of decline as droving faded before partial rescue came in the form of tourism in the south and, more recently, hydroelectric power schemes in the north. Even so, the road has, in many places, the air of remembering greater days. It carries only local traffic and, apart from day trippers to the Sma' Glen, seems not to be greatly favoured by tourists. The result is that although it is tarred the whole way, many stretches are eminently walkable.

The road had a part to play in both the opening phase and the last act of the Forty-Five. Cope's unhappy march north along it in August 1745 was mentioned in the last chapter. The following January, in the confused aftermath of the battle of Falkirk, it was decided to march the two divisions of the Jacobite army north in the hope of wintering quietly in the Highlands and regrouping in the spring. The disagreements which were to lead ultimately to the Jacobite defeat at Culloden had already become apparent, and after a heated council of war at Crieff on 2 February it was decided that Prince Charles would march with one division by way of Dalnacardoch while the other would take the coast road to Inverness. Once again, the King's enemies were making good use of the King's road.

Men in search of power start out by making it seem churlish that you should not follow them. They often end, as Charles Edward Stuart did, by making their followers shake their heads in disbelief at their own folly. At some point between August 1745 and February 1746 the symptoms of this change had appeared in the Prince. On the road from Glenfinnan, he had marched on foot with his men, eaten with them and slept with them. But since then he had been seduced by the delights of Blair Atholl, where he had stayed in state on his journey south. He had ridden into Edinburgh on his white horse. He had begun to feel like a Prince instead of merely a Pretender. And so, when he went north with his men in 1746, he had distanced himself from them. He was no longer on foot. He no longer saw in the march an opportunity for morale-building. While his men fared for themselves, he stayed at the inn at Amulree. Later on in the same march he forsook even inns and went out of his way to stop overnight at the houses of well-disposed nobles. As the march south six months before had seen his stature and regard grow, so, on the way from Crieff northwards, one can see the slow ebbing away of the Bonnie Prince Charlie charisma until he came, at last, to Culloden, a prince born to be spurned. So it was along the road that we are now going to explore that Charles Edward Stuart began his long ride into obscurity.

Wade's road left Crieff near the present Hydro, climbed the Knock of Crieff and headed northeast for Monzie, meeting the Shaggie Burn about a mile from the village. Beyond Monzie his track comes up from the left to meet the A822, which it follows as far as Foulford Inn. (I am told that the inn is famous for its high teas, for which people come from miles around.) Almost opposite the inn the Wade route leaves the A822 and strikes north along the lane leading to Connachan Lodge. From here, there is a pleasant and undemanding three-mile walk until old road and new meet again at Giant's Grave. The lane from the main road crosses a bridge and bears left to skirt some woodland. Shortly after this, immediately before a keeper's cottage, Wade's way goes sharp right through a gate and so north-

Hydroelectricity lines, Tummel Bridge

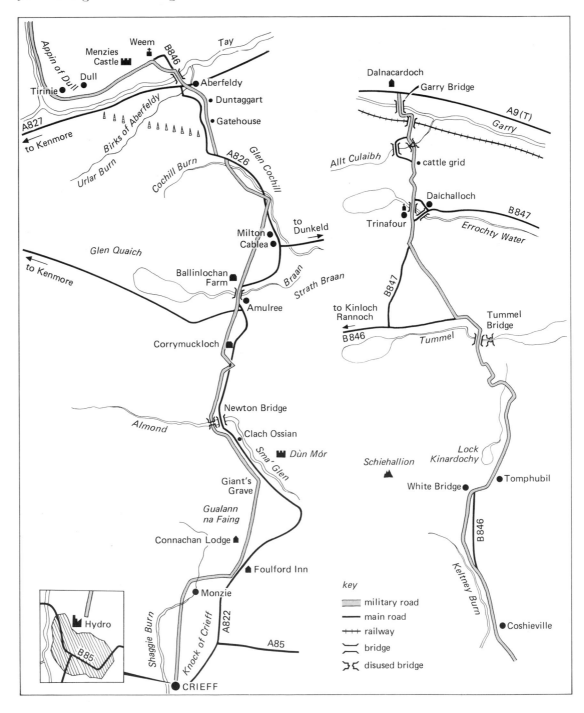

Corpses of trapped animals, Foulford Inn

ward. The track climbs quite steeply, and on a clear day it is worth turning round at the top for a splendid view south towards Loch Earn and Ben Vorlich. At the top, a Land Rover track leads right towards a gate in the plantation fence which is liberally hung with the corpses of vermin. Ignore this and take the lesser track leading straight ahead, keeping the plantation on your right. The sight and sound of the traffic in the glen are now lost, as the track leads over the shoulder of Gualann na Faing, across a stream, and so down into the Sma' Glen to rejoin the road. This walk is, incidentally, one that should be avoided between mid-August and mid-October, unless on a Sunday, because the area is very heavily shot.

The mile or so in the middle of the Sma' Glen, starting at Giant's Grave, is one of those areas that seem to attract the attention of folklorists and antiquarians. Overlooking it, on the summit of Dùn Mór, are the remains of an ancient fort (not accessible from this side). To the north, alongside the road, is Clach Ossian, said to be the burial place of the third century Gaelic poet whose credentials are in some doubt (see Chapter 5), and nearby is a grassy mound said (without supporting evidence) to be the grave of one of Wade's soldiers. It is not clear whether Ossian's stone is the stone told of in an anecdote of Edward Burt, but the incident certainly took place in this area. The road-builders came across a stone in their way 'of such an enormous size that it might be a matter of great wonder how it

Wade's road above Glen Almond

The Sma' Glen

could ever be removed by human strength and art.' Having moved it at last, they found underneath a hollow about two feet square in which were ashes, bones and half-burned stalks of heather 'which last we concluded to be a small remnant of a funeral pile'. Burt's opinion was that it was 'the urn of some considerable Roman officer', but investigation of the matter was frustrated by a party of Highlanders who gathered to collect the remains and take them to a new burial place.

The Sma' Glen has been and still is much admired. Dorothy Wordsworth, travelling through it in 1803, was enthusiastic: 'It is truly a solitude, the road even making it appear still more so: the bottom of the valley is mostly smooth and level, the brook not noisy: everything is simple and undisturbed, and while we passed through it the whole place was shady, cool, clear and solemn.' William, hearing of the legend of Ossian's stone, was moved to verse, but it was not one of his best days:

> In this still place remote from men
> Sleeps Ossian, in the Narrow Glen,
> In this still place where murmurs on
> But one meek streamlet, only one,

The Sma' Glen looking south

and so on for another twenty-eight lines. A considerable layby at Newton Bridge, with ice-cream vans and chip merchants in season, shows that the glen still attracts the traveller, though it is doubtful whether many these days come to tread in the footsteps of the Wordsworths.

Newton Bridge across the River Almond was built in the reconstruction of the 1820s, but just beyond it a now isolated Wade bridge marks the point at which the military road struck to the left, keeping more or less parallel to the present road for about two boggy miles. Then, on a right-hand bend, it briefly crosses to the right of the new road, recrosses it, runs to the west of the farmstead of Corrymuckloch and then heads in an almost straight line for Amulree. This stretch can be walked but, again, at the southern end it is inclined to be boggy. At the Amulree end, it heads down the slope, making direct for the former schoolhouse, its line clearly marked with two parallel lines of boulders and looking not unlike a miniature version of West Kennet Avenue near Avebury. Marker stones were an essential finishing touch to Wade's roads, especially on slopes as exposed as this one, and they were early versions of the red and white striped marker posts to be found today along Highland roads. Where the avenue meets the road it is securely fenced off (a carload of locals stared hard while I was pondering whether to climb over) but there is a useful gate at the corner of the village hall car park.

Amulree seems to have come into being as a creature of the droving trade at the turn of the eighteenth century. No fewer than four arterial drove roads converged there: from Kenmore down Glen Quaich, from Dalnacardoch along the route substantially adopted by Wade, from Ballinluig by Loch Skiach (a fearsomely exposed route that no one other than drovers has ever dared to regularize), and from Dunkeld by way of Strath Braan. As the last stopping place before Crieff, it naturally built up a subsidiary market trade from buyers who were prepared to travel twelve miles on from the main

Wade's road near Amulree

market and from drovers ready to save a day's travelling provided the price was right. By Wade's time there was a substantial trade in cattle and sheep, deals being agreed by a handshake between buyer and seller over a boulder in the yard at Corrymuckloch. With the building of the kirk, magnificently sited on a knoll overlooking the village, in 1744, Amulree must have felt that it was truly on the map.

In fact, by that time it had already made a footnote in history. In 1715, there was an assembly of clans on their way to the Earl of Mar's great gathering at Braemar which signalled the start of the Fifteen, and Amulree was no doubt chosen for the same reason as gave it significance on the drovers' map. The main body of the present hotel building carries the date 1714 (which would be about right for an inn for the droving trade). As noted earlier, Prince Charles spent the night there on his march north in 1746.

Although the railway never reached Amulree, the village seems to have adapted itself well to changing times. As the droving trade

The hotel at Amulree

Glen Cochill

dwindled and could no longer support a village smithy, tourism took over, drawn mainly by the fishing in Loch Freuchie, and the inn was described in the guidebooks as 'small but comfortable'. In summer, it was the lodging for gentlemen from Oxford and Cambridge, and their ladies, who assembled at Amulree for reading parties under the guidance of Annie Swann, the minor Victorian novelist who was schoolmistress there and wrote some of her books in the schoolhouse. It is pleasant to think of these civilized and cultured people travelling several hundred miles to commune with literature, earnestly discussing points as they sat under their parasols on the lawn behind the inn which, though only roughly cut these days, was clearly once neatly landscaped. Later still, Amulree adapted to the motoring age, the inn's spacious stables turned into garages, and the inn itself taking on the slightly raffish air which it still has. It is not hard to imagine the early roadsters rolling down from Corrymuckloch, to disembark leather-coated and heavily goggled figures (bounders to a man, and their ladies not their wives nor likely to be) banging their hands together for warmth and then unstrapping the suitcases from the running boards. Cheerfully, Amulree has accepted them all – drovers, soldiers, clansmen, literati, bounders – and deserves to be admired for it.

Wade headed north across a predecessor of the present bridge and then, almost at once, turned north through the yard of Ballinlochan Farm along a line, still distinguishable in part but impossible to pursue, to the west of Cablea and Milton, crossing and recrossing the A826 through metal gates between one and two miles north of Milton. You would need to be a dedicated Wade-follower to walk the twelve miles or so between Amulree and Aberfeldy. Glen Cochill is dull country, afflicted with the kind of afforestation that has given the Forestry Commission a bad name – though it is to be doubted whether anything much more interesting could have been done with this undistinguished stretch of bleak moorland. After crossing the Cochill Burn about five miles south of Aberfeldy, Wade's track comes into the main road from the left, crosses it and is then lost in new forestry works. It re-emerges about two miles farther on as the track leading to Gatehouse on the right side of the A826 and follows the road as far as the drive to Duntaggart, where it veers off to the right as the main road curves away left. The way now is downhill along a line of trees and down a path beside some cottages to emerge at Cottage Hospital Lane. This in turn becomes the Old Crieff Road and joins the main square at Aberfeldy near the Co-op Stores.

Aberfeldy, built around Wade's bridge, was a town virtually created by him. The drovers had crossed the Tay about two miles to the west, towards Kenmore. Their road continued northwest where Wade's turns sharply north about a mile before Gatehouse, crossed the Urlar Burn above the Birks of Aberfeldy, celebrated in one of Burns's poems, and dropped down to the Tay, making the crossing somewhere near the village of Dull. A line of electricity pylons follows their course almost exactly.

Wade was proud of his Tay Bridge at Aberfeldy, and from the beginning invested care in its planning. It is certainly the least utilitarian of his bridges in appearance, reflecting the fact that he engaged William Adam, elder brother of the better-known Robert, but Scotland's leading architect of the time, to design it. To ensure an early start as soon as the weather permitted in 1733, stores were

The Tay valley as it descends from Glen Cochill, looking northeast

brought to the site the previous year, and Adam sent to the north of England for suitably experienced carpenters and masons. The first stone was laid on 23 April 1733, and Wade paid close attention to the work that summer, staying at the inn at Weem, one mile up the road towards Coshieville. By mid-August, when he conducted an official inspection, the major work was over and, although the finishing touches were left until the next year, the bridge was usable that winter.

The luxuries that Wade permitted himself at Tay Bridge, distinguishing it from others, were the four obelisks over the main span and the two laudatory tablets, in Latin and English, set beneath two of them. The present ones, incidentally, are copies of the originals made in 1932; the originals were placed on the outside of the obelisks. The wording is interesting, partly for the contrast between the heroic style of the Latin and the more pedestrian English but also because, in the English version, the purpose of Wade's roads is claimed to be commercial rather than military. Latin scholars are invited to

Admire this military road, extending two hundred and fifty miles beyond the frontier of the Romans, jumping across wastes and marshes and spanning the angry Tay. This arduous undertaking was completed in the year 1733 by G. Wade, Commander of the Forces in Scotland, by his skill and the labour of his soldiers for ten years.

This is all a bit woolly as to facts – it did not take ten years to bridge the angry Tay, for example – but the more modest English version records the erection of the bridge in 1733 and Wade's responsibility for 'the roads and other military works for securing a safe and easy communication between the high lands and the tradeing towns in the low country.' It has to be admitted that, despite their aversion to roads, the drovers abandoned their traditional route after the Tay Bridge was built and took advantage of Wade's work.

Compared with the functional simplicity of Wade's other bridges, the Tay Bridge looks rather overplayed. Dorothy Wordsworth thought it 'a bridge of ambitious and ugly architecture', and a modern commentator on the historic architecture of Scotland, J. G. Dunbar, is not exactly overenthusiastic in noting it as 'an elaborate structure of some architectural distinction', adding that 'such refinement of design is unusual in public bridges at this period'. However, the burghers of Aberfeldy have made the most of it, laying out a pleasant riverside garden which also takes in the Black Watch Memorial, erected in 1887 as a Jubilee offering to Queen Victoria. This commemorates the formation at Aberfeldy in 1739 of the six independent companies of Highland troops, the Black Watch, which was one of the steps Wade had recommended fifteen years before for the repression of the lawless Highlanders.

From Aberfeldy onwards Wade's road becomes a B road and is pleasant walking as far as Dalnacardoch, if a little dull for the first five miles or so to Coshieville. You can choose from a variety of base camps: a wide range of hotels and guest houses in Aberfeldy, the Weem Hotel, which was Wade's base in 1733 and has a portrait of him over the door, a guest house at Tirinie or the Coshieville Hotel, a former drovers' inn which Wade took over as a barracks for his working-parties. If your taste runs that way, you can even hire a bicycle at Coshieville.

The Tay Bridge, Aberfeldy

Wade left Aberfeldy along a line whose beginnings can be distinguished but which is now impassable. It bears to the left at the northern end of Tay Bridge and sweeps round in a curve, rejoining the B846 opposite Weem church. Menzies Castle, on your right on the way out of Weem, is a grand pile built in 1571, gradually being restored by the Menzies clan as a voluntary labour of love and loyalty. It is yet another of the places that put up Prince Charles in 1745, not to mention Mary Queen of Scots at an earlier date. After a steepish climb alongside the Keltney Burn from Coshieville, the road swings away to the right and Wade's way was to the left of the present road, running behind the caravan and camping site and rejoining the B846 at White Bridge. Now the country opens out, and from here on as far as the descent to Tummel Bridge the view to the left is dominated by the 3547-foot peak of Schiehallion, a distinctive cone shape some five miles to the west.

About half a mile farther on, above the road to the right, is what looks as if it might be a relic of Wade's time – a substantial structure with a commanding view across Loch Kinardochy towards the Tummel. In fact, it has nothing at all to do with Wade, but throws some light on the economics of Scotland after the Forty-Five. Agricultural improvement was the order of the day, in the hope of raising the desperately poor yields of Scottish farmers and growers. Prodigious quantities of lime were needed, and it was found and

Wade's bridge, Tummel Bridge

Tummel Bridge

quarried in the Tomphubil area. Only the existence of Wade's road – and, later, the improvements of the Commissioners for Highland Roads and Bridges – would have made it feasible to transport lime from this fairly remote spot. The kiln itself was built in the mid-nineteenth century and continued in use until the early 1900s, by which time, no doubt, lime could more economically be brought in by rail from easier sources.

Tummel Bridge, reached by a long and winding descent, illustrates a more recent phase of economic development. This settlement, like the next one going north on the Wade road, Trinafour, isolated and with few resources, would no doubt by now be a collection of roofless cottages but for the North of Scotland Hydroelectric Board, 'the hydro' as it is more usually called. The supply station at Tummel Bridge was built in the 1930s under private enterprise and without much regard for the environment; it dominates the place, and the ruinous effect has been compounded by the gaunt metal bridge which has been placed alongside, and obscures, Wade's bridge of 1733. 'Placed' is perhaps not the word; it looks as if it were flung down one weekend by an inexperienced party of Royal Engineer reservists, and forgotten. The addition of the grossly out-of-scale Tummel Bridge Holiday Park (fifteen holiday chalets and seventy-five caravans which will, with any luck, one day be better screened than they are today) completes the spoilation of what must have been, up to fifty years ago, one of the Highlands' most peaceful places.

This is the dilemma of development. Wade's bridge could never have taken the occasional heavy hydro loads that pass this way. The hydro and, to a lesser extent, the holiday park provide jobs in an area that needs every one. But the argument goes on. Once built, hydro schemes employ only a handful of people; the benefits go mainly to the industrial centres of the south. It was estimated in 1968 that only about 2000 new jobs had been created in the Highlands by the hydro board's scheme to encourage industrial consumers to set up shop locally. But then, how would a light industrial estate look at Tummel Bridge? As for the holiday park, it is a perfect illustration of the argument of the Scottish Vigilantes Association in 1964 that 'the Highlands are not in a position to appeal to the tourist mass market owing to the limited facilities, and furthermore ... to do so would result in visitors in search of quiet and solitude being discouraged.'

The next ten miles, north of Tummel Bridge, are a delight, however. After a steep climb through woodland, the road opens out as it clings to the hillside, with superb views to the west and Schiehallion dominating the south. Then follows a slow descent to the junction with the B847 from Kinloch Rannoch and, a mile farther on, Trinafour. This, too, is a village kept alive by the hydro – Loch Errochty, to the west, is dammed – but the attendant works are low and neatly tucked away at the north end of the village. Trinafour is a little gem of a place, hidden in a lush, warm valley which is the more of a surprise for coming so soon after the high, open walk from Tummel Bridge. The first building you reach is the post office, deeply scented by the old roses in the postmistress's garden next door. (She also sells pop and crisps, but nothing more serious.) Shortly after this, the present road bears right to cross the Errochty Water at Dalchalloch. Wade's road went straight on (follow the signpost to the church) down a shrub-lined lane and over the Errochty Water, rejoining the new road in front of the former kingshouse and inn, cosily sited with its back to the hillside. It is worth a diversion to look at the church, sited in a nest of rhododendrons and honeysuckle with a curious porch got up in Ruritanian hunting lodge style.

The longer way through Trinafour, by the new road, is also worth taking, if only to admire the surprising variety of trees – oak, ash, birch, sycamore and rowan as well as various conifers – and, on the north side of the stream, the curiosity of a bus shelter with a gate to keep out the sheep. I couldn't help wondering just how many buses stop here; there was no sign of a timetable, but doubtless there are few enough for the inhabitants of Trinafour to know them by heart. Nearby, under the trees, is a good picnic spot beside the water, but you need to be well lathered with anti-midge cream.

Sleepy and quiet though it is now (and long may it remain so), Trinafour was a hive of activity in the droving days. Roughly ten miles – a day's droving – from Dalnacardoch to the north and Tummel Bridge, it was an overnight stopping place, and doubtless the inn enjoyed a good trade in the month or so before the Crieff

Beinn a' Chuallaich

Wade's road north of Tummel Bridge

tryst. Like Amulree, it had a smithy for the shoeing of cattle. This practice became commonplace after the military roads were built, allegedly because the gravel wore down the hooves; but it was a crude business compared with the shoeing of horses, thin metal plates being nailed to the outer edges of the hooves, and the shoes might have to be renewed several times in the course of a drove from the Highlands to, say, Norfolk where most Scottish cattle were fattened for the London market. In the mid-nineteenth century the Trinafour smithy was run by a Kennedy family, and the building can still be seen on the north bank of the Errochty Water about fifty yards along the new road from Wade's bridge.

Another steep climb takes you past the modest hydro installation and into a series of zigzags almost as exhausting as those on the Corrieyairack, except that here there is the benefit of a tarred road surface. The views south and west provide plenty of excuses to stop for a rest. The road rises to over 1400 feet, and there's a satisfying sense of space and wide skies from here until, just after the cattle grid, the descent to Dalnacardoch begins. Here, Wade went straight on where the modern road turns to the left, followed the left bank of the Allt Culaibh and crossed it over a bridge whose remains are still visible. This way is passable but rough going. Farther on, the railway bridge somewhat obscures the original Wade line, but you pick it up again just before the Garry bridge, which is original Wade. Dalnacardoch, hardly noticed now by people who flash by in the train or on the new A9, was a place of some importance to travellers until the end of the nineteenth century. Wade built one of his 'huts' here, and it was later expanded into a patrol post with a sergeant in charge. With the withdrawal of the military from the Highlands, Dalnacardoch Lodge became an inn, and in coaching days was a famous stopping place for coaches on the Inverness to Perth run. The railway killed this trade, but the house found a new role as a shooting lodge, as it has remained. At the same time, Dalnacardoch was on the drovers' map and, significantly and pleasingly, there is a yard of modern stock pens in the area beside the railway where drovers used to rest their sheep and cattle overnight.

When Prince Charles's division of the Jacobite army arrived at Dalnacardoch from Crieff – and a cold coming they must have had of it, for it was early February and from Tummel Bridge, except for the brief respite at Trinafour, it is as exposed a road as any in Scotland – they met the baggage and artillery train which had been coming up from Perth through the Killiecrankie Pass. Culloden was still two months away, but as the Prince struggled through the snow across Drumochter, towards the fateful last act of his adventure, anyone less self-centred must surely have realized that this was the beginning of the end.

5
The Great Highland Road

In terms of endurance, the road from Dunkeld to Inverness was Wade's greatest achievement. Just over 100 miles long, it was driven through Killiecrankie, over the Drumochter Pass, across the great moorland of Speyside and through the dreaded Slochd. It is a tribute to Wade's choice of route (though in some places, as at Killiecrankie, he had little choice) that it was largely adhered to when Telford came to build his road north in the early years of the nineteenth century, by the builders of the Highland Railway in the early 1860s, and even, to a large extent, despite their sophisticated excavating and road-building equipment, by the planners of the new A9 which is gradually replacing Telford's road. Nevertheless, the successive overlayings of all these contractors has rendered much of Wade's road either undistinguished or indistinguishable, and as a monument it is less impressive than, say, the Corrieyairack road or the great upland sweep between Tummel Bridge and Dalnacardoch described in the previous chapter. Almost all of it can be traced, but for long stretches it coincides with the modern road, which is the main route for Inverness and the north, and so is hardly comfortable for walkers. Perhaps about a quarter of Wade's original line, broken down into fairly short lengths, makes enjoyable walking.

It took three seasons, from 1728 to 1730, to complete the Highland Road. In planning his routes from Crieff to Dalnacardoch and from Dalwhinnie to Fort Augustus, Wade followed the drovers, perhaps having reasoned, despite his initial reservations, that it was best to listen to the wisdom of generations that had created the drove roads. Working from Dunkeld to Inverness, however, he was more adventurous. For some twenty miles, between Ballinluig and Dalnacardoch, he struck out on his own, crossing the vast Atholl estates and, incidentally, linking the two main arteries of the drove road system which ran southwards from Aviemore by way of Glen Feshie and Glen Fearnach to Kirkmichael and so on to Amulree, and from Dalnacardoch to Amulree along the route described in Chapter

4. In doing so, he unwittingly settled the future of communications in this part of Scotland, though he did not settle the arguments, for there are those who still maintain that a route through Glen Feshie and Glen Fearnach would be better for all-weather travel. Whenever there is any new development in the air (as, for example, when the 'improved' A9 was planned) the rival claims still scorch the letters columns of Scottish newspapers. However, the die was cast nearly 250 years ago by Wade. There were good reasons why the drovers should have avoided Blair Atholl and the Tay crossing at Dunkeld, and why Wade should have taken his road that way. Drovers were not welcome in the decorous surroundings of Blair, and at Dunkeld there was a toll. But it was important for Wade to keep an eye on Atholl. The first Duke, who died in 1724, had remained loyal in the Fifteen, but three of his sons had favoured the Jacobites; and indeed, as we have seen, the second Duke, who had been in exile since 1715, returned to Scotland with Prince Charles and played a part, if only as a figurehead, in the raising of the Jacobite standard at Glenfinnan in 1745. Wade may also have been influenced by the fact that there was already a rudimentary military road system through Blair Atholl, and in the immediate environs of the castle he could make a useful economy by adopting the estate roads as a basis for his own.

The work began in the summer of 1728 with three hundred men deployed in two parties, one working south from Inverness and the other north from Dunkeld. The project evidently went well, for in October of the following year Wade wrote of having travelled by coach from Ruthven Barracks near Kingussie to Dalnaspidal, over the Drumochter Pass, 'with great ease and pleasure' to a feast prepared by the road-builders. A tent was pitched for the meal, and four oxen were roasted, and there was plenty to drink. After three hours of this, Wade rode south to his 'hut' at Dalnacardoch, where he was to begin the survey of his projected road to Crieff.

The road from Dunkeld began with a ferry across the Tay at Inver, about a mile upstream from the present bridge, which was built in the early 1800s with a handsome subsidy from the Duke of Atholl in return for the proceeds of a toll. (Since he owned the ferry rights, he was not giving much away.) The track can be traced on the east bank of the river as an estate road passing Dunkeld House (in those days a dower house) and leading north to join the present A9 about five miles out of Dunkeld. From here as far as Blair Atholl, with only trivial diversions, the modern road follows and obliterates Wade.

The Wordsworths passed this way in 1803 – William bestowing a sonnet at Killiecrankie – but, although dutifully impressed with the Duke of Atholl's gardens on the west bank at Dunkeld, they were ill served at Faskally, just south of Killiecrankie. Twilight was coming on, and they were fearful of going through Killiecrankie after dark. The only inn gave William whisky by the fire, but refused them beds for the night. The landlady was too tired, she said. So they went on through Killiecrankie after all, 'hearing only the roaring of the river and seeing a black chasm with jagged-topped black hills towering above', according to Dorothy. At Blair Atholl, though alarmed by drunkards from a nearby fair, they were 'civilly treated'. It's not too easy, it must be said, to reconcile Dorothy Wordsworth's picture of Killiecrankie with the tourist trap of today, with its information centre, nature trails, caravan site and Little Chef restaurantette.

J. B. Salmond, who investigated the Blair Atholl area fairly thoroughly in the 1930s, said that Wade's route through Blair was across the Old Bridge of Tilt, through Old Blair and so to Baluain, where it joined the A9, thus taking travellers to the north of Blair Castle. Following this cue, William Taylor, in the 1970s, constructed a possible route through Old Blair, but Wade's line here is not certain. The estate itself has changed a good deal since Wade's day, and in addition it seems likely that the coming of the railway, changing the emphasis hereabouts to the area round what is now the Atholl Arms Hotel, changed the structure of the road system.

Pitagowan, two miles farther on, marks the point where Wade departed from the traditional military route to the north. This lay over the Minigaig Pass and so into the rival Glen Feshie system. Thanks to the Scottish Rights of Way Society, this route is still walkable from Calvine, one mile west of Pitagowan, to near Ruthven Barracks, a distance of some thirty miles. It is a demanding march, rising to 2745 feet – some 1250 feet higher than Drumochter – and although it is not part of our present agenda, since it predates Wade and was not adopted by him, it can be recommended as a summer excursion for walkers with good boots, a compass and satisfactory arrangements for transport or accommodation at the other end. The compass is necessary because for two or three longish stretches the

path disappears and has to be divined by reference to points forward. The Minigaig Pass route, first mapped in the late seventeenth century, continued to be used by the military after Wade's time as a summer short cut to Ruthven, lopping ten miles off the journey, but it was even more vulnerable to snow blockage than the dreaded Drumochter.

Past Calvine, a four-mile stretch of Wade road marches a few hundred yards above the A9, with two Wade bridges, but this seems destined to be overlaid by the line of the improved trunk road. The new roadworks have also done for what remained of two Wade diversions near Dalnacardoch, where the Crieff road comes in from the left. At the very threshold of Drumochter, near Dalnaspidal, is the site of the feast mentioned earlier in this chapter, and Wade-fanciers may find it worthwhile to park in Dalnaspidal itself, brave the fast-moving traffic on the new trunk road and plod about a quarter of a mile upstream to where the ruined Oxbridge marks the spot. From here, the Wade alignment can be followed for about a mile and a half, above the new road, until it is lost again at the point where the new dual carriageway ends. The Pass of Drumochter itself, forbidding enough even to the motorist in winter, as evidenced by the snow gates at each end, is better driven than walked, and most Wade remnants have disappeared. But it is worth turning off to the left just after the northern snow gate to look at the Wade bridge carrying his road over the Truim to follow its west bank along the line now taken by the railway, to emerge as Ben Allder Road leading to Dalwhinnie station.

For all that it is the home of Long John whisky, Dalwhinnie is a desperate place, one of the contenders, surely, for the title of the ugliest village in the Highlands. Its coldness and bleakness are legendary. Both my visits have been in August, and even then it was impossible not to agree with Murray's 1894 *Handbook for Scotland*, which describes Dalwhinnie as 'a desolate and solitary spot, protected by a few fir-trees from the cold winds'. It must have been a cheerless stopover for the drovers, especially since they had the cold comfort of Drumochter to face next day. It is piquant to think that the drivers of the cattle wagons who stop for double egg, bacon and chips at one of Dalwhinnie's numerous transport cafés may be the descendants of the drovers who, having settled their beasts on the pastures beside the Truim, wound themselves into their plaids against the Dalwhinnie winds with a dram or two inside them for extra warmth.

From here, the road over Corrieyairack described in Chapter 3 branches away to the west. Now that the new A9 from Dalwhinnie northwards has been rebuilt on the east bank of the Truim, the older road on the west bank is once again suitable for walking, with only an occasional vehicle. Past the Long John distillery (open to visitors in the season, but closed for maintenance in August) the present A889 for Spean Bridge curves to the left to cross the railway. The Wade line kept straight on at this corner and joined the old main road about half a mile beyond the junction; the first part of this alignment can be seen clearly, but the railway prevents its being followed all the way.

There is something particularly attractive, it seems to me, about the old A9, probably because it remained in use from Wade's time until very recently, and it is appealing to think of its 250 years' experience of traffic, from horse and foot through cart and coach to the day of the juggernaut. It must be quieter now than it has been for at least fifty years. Approaching Crubenmore Lodge, however, three different alignments appear west of the Truim. Wade forked left at this point, keeping to the left of the Truim, and his track can be followed along the lower slopes of Crùban Beag, following the river round until it suddenly takes a southward turn for the bridge, and so to rejoin the old A9. The most modern of the three alignments forges ahead across the Truim shortly after Crubenmore Lodge at Crubenmore Bridge, but to the right an older road, the Telford alignment, curves round a cottage at the west end of the newer bridge, makes its own crossing across two arches and runs alongside the railway before rejoining the road after about 200 yards. So here, within about a hundred yards of each other, we have five generations of transport in Scotland: Wade, Telford, a more recent alignment, probably of the 1930s, the Highland Railway, opened in 1863, and, on the east side, the new A9.

The bridge over the Truim at Crubenbeg was the junction with the spur road to Catlodge and Laggan. There is a mystery about this road, since there is no reference to it in Wade's reports except for one or two oblique phrases which might, or might not, be relevant. Such a road certainly existed, and it enabled Cope to make his retreat from the Corrieyairack to Ruthven in 1745. It is equally certain that there is today a track which can be followed from Crubenbeg northwards as far as the electricity pylons and then west until it picks up a minor road leading to Catlodge. Among dedicated Wade-watchers, the line taken by the spur road, and indeed its very existence, is a point of hot debate in which the word 'controversy' has even been heard. The fundamentalists, finding nothing in Wade's own records, will have nothing of conjectural alignments; the freethinkers, however, seem even to the amateur to be stretching a point or two here and there. All that can be said with certainty is that there was a way that Cope could take to reach Ruthven from Sherramore without going south to Dalwhinnie; and there the amateur would be wise to leave the matter.

There is, however, ahead of us a walk of some eight miles which is undisputedly Wade. It begins at a gate immediately opposite the turning to the Wade bridge at Crubenbeg, where a track leads along

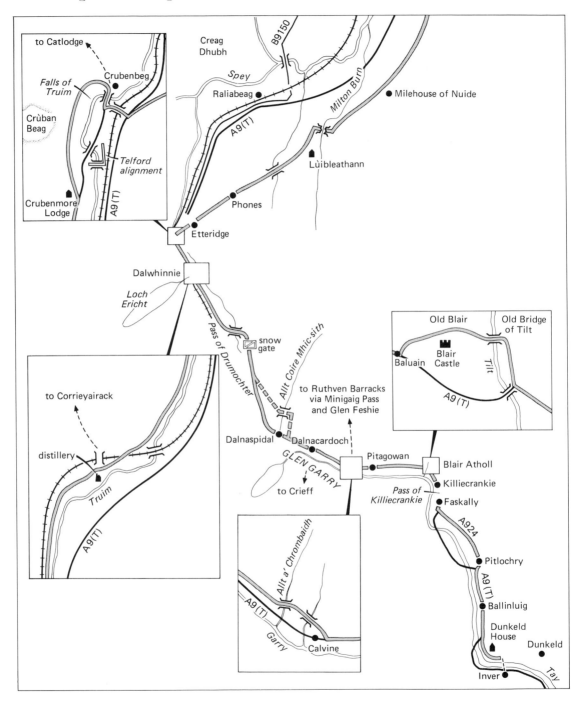

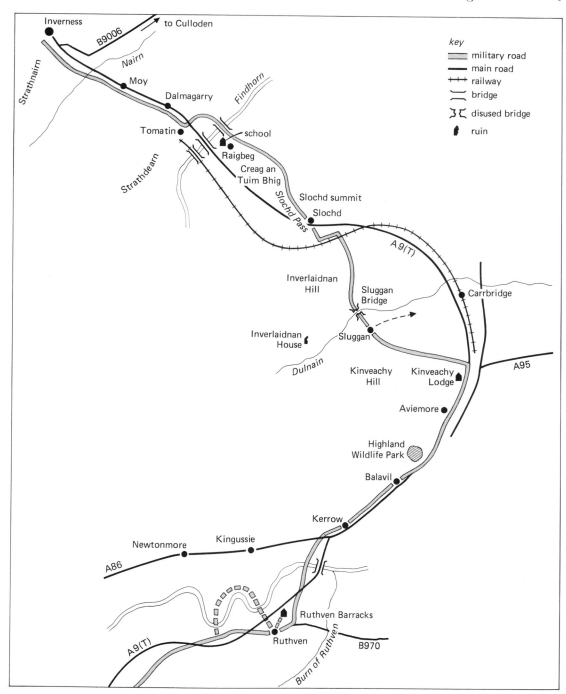

key
military road
main road
railway
bridge
disused bridge
ruin

Inverness
B9006
to Culloden
Nairn
Strathnairn
Moy
Dalmagarry
Findhorn
Tomatin
school
Strathdearn
Raigbeg
Creag an
Tuim Bhig
Slochd summit
Slochd Pass
Slochd
A9(T)
Inverlaidnan
Hill
Carrbridge
Sluggan
Bridge
Inverlaidnan
House
Sluggan
Dulnain
A95
Kinveachy
Hill
Kinveachy
Lodge
Aviemore
Highland
Wildlife Park
Balavil
Kerrow
Newtonmore
Kingussie
A86
Ruthven Barracks
A9(T)
Ruthven
Burn of Ruthven
B970

the lower edge of woodland towards Etteridge. There is parking space in a cul-de-sac which was part of the old A9, just over the bridge beyond the Falls of Truim before the old road meets the new. After about half a mile, the track joins a metalled surface coming in from the left at Etteridge, and from here on as far as Phones the Wade line follows the farm road. Beyond Phones, the track gradually peters out while remaining, for most of the way, clear enough. First there is a delightful grassy area on the edge of birchwoods, a very Scottish setting with well-drained alpine pasture. As there are few sheltered spots over the next five miles, this is an ideal picnic spot. The grassy shelf is crossed by parallel tracks, of which the westward is probably the original Wade line. However, this leads to a boggy patch, and it is probably best to keep towards the birch trees and pick up the old alignment again near the gate at the far end. On the south side of the gate is one of Wade's original waymarks, and about 250 paces farther on, on the left, is what is almost certainly a grave, unmarked in the heather.

Although the way ahead is along Land Rover tracks which have clearly been maintained for estate purposes, the next three miles or so bring the walker very close to what it must have been like to march a Wade road in the days when it existed for military business and not leisure. There are no pylons, even, to disturb the effect, and the traffic noise from the A9 is a mile or more away. This stretch of road, from Etteridge almost to Ruthven Barracks, was in fact in military use for only about thirty years, having been superseded in 1763 by a road along the line of the now superannuated B970 to Ralia, and so to Etteridge. Perhaps this accounts for the old road's remarkable preservation: few people have wanted to come this way for over 200 years, electricity board men included.

The track now leads across what must have been one of Wade's easier marches, across a well-drained landscape with few boulders. How, after their earlier trials, his men must have fairly skipped along here – and so may we – though in winter it cannot have taken many snow flurries to obscure the road completely, and perhaps this was the reason for finding a new alignment in the shelter of Creag Dhubh and the Spey. Isolated in the middle of the plain, visible for a long way in each direction, is Wade's bridge over one of the Spey's tributaries, a modest but perfect example. At the top of the rise from the bridge, going north, a confusion of paths crosses the basin, and some care is needed to pick out the Wade line, which leads from gate to gate with Lùibleathan Cottage kept on the right, following what appears to be the lesser of the two paths. Beyond Lùibleathan, the road curves to the right and dips to cross the Milton Burn.

It looks as if there was once a bridge here, but it has been lost. A trunk has been lashed in place for the crossing, but for those who don't fancy such assault-course tactics there is an easier crossing over the rocks some 400 yards upstream where the water is quieter. With the open moorland left behind, there is another change of flora. The path leads past a row of four abandoned cottages (though the sheepfank beside them has been in use more recently) and along a shelf rich (in August) in rockrose, alpine bedstraw, violets, knapweed, clover, short yarrow, eyebright, scabious, harebells, boletus, thyme and birdsfoot trefoil. About half a mile from the Milton Burn crossing is the Milehouse of Nuide, obviously once a substantial settlement stretching for about 300 yards along the track. A curious circular lochan marks the beginning of a succession of remnants which become more easy to pick out as one goes north. At the northern end was an enclosure some 120 yards long, stretching back almost the same distance from the road, in which the outlines of two or three buildings can be traced.

The track leads on clearly enough through a plantation and then curves to the left towards the new A9. Approaching this road, a Land Rover track curves to the right to meet an access gap in the main road fencing, but Wade's line is clearly decipherable, going straight on towards an electricity pylon where it meets the B970 and ultimately the A9. It is interesting, incidentally, that the new road takes the south side of the Spey at this point, perhaps vindicating Wade's original choice.

The main road crossing is no problem with normal caution, and the line is picked up again at the stile at the top of the embankment on the left-hand side. The track here has been overlaid by roadworks, but over the crest it is picked up again as a metalled road (the B970) which follows the east bank of the Spey for about 200 yards. From here, Wade's approach to Ruthven Barracks is in some doubt. There is only one way to go now, which is along the road, through the subway under the new A9 and along the metalled road to what remains of Ruthven village. This avoids a river crossing, and it would seem sensible for Wade to have taken this route also; but

Ruthven Barracks

Opposite:
*Northeast from
Ruthven Barracks*

there is a suggestion that just short of the subway he crossed the Spey and approached Ruthven along what is now the north bank of the river, necessitating another crossing below the barracks. A lot can happen to the course of a river in 250 years, and it may well be that in his day the Spey had not yet developed its two meanders at this point, in which case Wade could have taken the more direct route without crossing the river.

Ruthven Barracks were built between 1716 and 1721, before Wade was summoned to Scotland, and it is possible that if he had had the choice he would have built them somewhere else. But the site, a commanding mound which is said to be at least partly man-made, almost chose itself, having been a fortification since at least the fourteenth century. Ruthven itself was, in Wade's time, a substantial settlement occupying the area between the barracks and the junction of the Kingussie and Etteridge roads. Little of this remains. The two townships of significance now in this area, Kingussie and Newtonmore, were virtually creations of the railway

and the summer trade it brought, but apart from Ruthven the other important area hereabouts was at Pitmain, between the two. This was the scene of a sizeable cattle fair each September where cattle from the north were sold to drovers who would take them on to Crieff or, later, Falkirk.

Despite its rough treatment in the Forty-Five, Ruthven is still in good enough condition to give the visitor some idea of what it might have been like to be stationed there. It was originally intended to house a company of infantry, though it seems never to have been occupied to capacity, being used mainly as a patrol post with a small garrison. The stable block on the west side was added in 1734 and could accommodate up to thirty dragoons.

When Cope declined to meet Prince Charles's army at the Corrieyairack, he made for Inverness by way of Ruthven and reached the barracks on 27 August 1745. Here, the Ruthven garrison of infantry was added to the column, leaving only a Sergeant Molloy and a dozen men stationed there. Four days later, Ruthven was attacked by a force of three hundred Jacobites, whereupon Sergeant Molloy (who was later commissioned for his bravery) provided one of the few examples of commendable soldiering on the English side at this stage of the rebellion, successfully defending Ruthven with his twelve disciples.

Ruthven was to figure twice more in the story of the Forty-Five. Molloy was still in charge when, on their way north in 1746, heading for the fateful meeting at Culloden, another three-hundred-strong force of Jacobites, with artillery, called for Ruthven's surrender. Molloy had little choice, but managed to obtain safe conduct to Blair Atholl for himself and his men. Having gained Ruthven, the Jacobites burned it before moving on, but within a few days some of them were back. After Culloden, one arm of the Prince's dispirited and shattered army gathered at Ruthven, perhaps in the hope of rehabilitating it as a stronghold. But they were short of food and their morale was low, and they chose instead to disperse into the surrounding hills. One of them, Cluny Macpherson, was to stay in hiding in the mountains above Newtonmore for seven years. He was lucky; others who had chosen to flee to more accessible areas were hunted down in the reign of terror mounted by 'Butcher' Cumberland.

Wade's route to the north of Ruthven is not now traceable, but it went due north towards the river before turning northeast to follow the bank. The road left the the ferry on the west bank of the river by way of the present Manse Road in Kingussie, where there was an inn, Tigh-na-Coit, for the refreshment of passengers. This, described by one authority as a 'tiny dram-shop', evidently survived until the 1930s, when J. B. Salmond described it as an 'Old Road House'.

The Wade line now crosses the present main road and then leads through Kerrow approximately along the 800-foot contour, emerging at Balavil. From here on for about twenty miles, the combined efforts of modern road-building and the tourist industry have all but eliminated traces of Wade's road, but Balavil is the source of two footnotes in Scottish history, one long before Wade and the other shortly after. The first explains why this area has a reputation, somewhat surprising to the modern visitor, of wildness and savagery. Balavil House is built on the site of the Castle of Raits, the scene of one of the clan slaughters with which early Scottish history is riddled. The Comyns, who had built the castle, invited their rivals, the Mackintoshes, to dinner, members of the two clans being placed alternately at table. The entry of the boar's head was to be the signal for each Comyn to kill his neighbour; but the Mackintoshes got wind of the plan, and when the boar's head came in took the cue first. Another tribute to Scottish hospitality. It is perhaps not surprising that the scene of this incident should have been chosen by James Macpherson, the fabricator of the Ossian translations, as the site of his Scottish seat. The dark Gaelishness of its history would have appealed to him.

Macpherson was born in Ruthven in 1736, and taught there for a while. He became interested in Gaelic literature, and in 1760 published his first collection of translations. This book included, in the manner of the day, an invitation to readers to subscribe towards the research into and translation of Ossian's *Fingal*, an epic poem of daunting length. Subscriptions were easily raised, and in December 1761 the translation appeared in six volumes. Further translations of Ossian followed.

After the Forty-Five, Scotland was thirsty for a boost to its morale, and the wider circulation of what appeared to be a genuine early literature was welcomed. In London, however, Dr Johnson and others had their suspicions, and it was partly to investigate Macpherson's claims that his works were translations and not inventions that Johnson made his celebrated tour of the Highlands and Western Isles in 1773. He pursued his inquiries with a degree of thoroughness which suggests an obsession, and he returned convinced that the Ossian translations were fakes. 'I look upon Macpherson's *Fingal*,' the doctor remarked, coming it a bit as usual, 'to be as gross an imposition as ever the world was troubled with. Had it been really an ancient work, a true specimen how men thought at that time, it would have been a curiosity of the first rate. As a modern production, it is nothing.' He added that he could write an epic poem about Robin Hood and 'half England, to whom the names and places he should mention in it are familiar, would believe and declare they had heard it from their earliest years.' This was a nasty crack at some of the expert witnesses he had interviewed in the Highlands and Islands, who had made just that claim about *Fingal*.

James Macpherson, challenged to produce the Gaelic originals of

his translations, never did so, and a succession of scholars of Scottish literature eventually, after the controversy had raged for a century, satisfied themselves that *Fingal* and the rest were of Macpherson's own invention. It was one of the literary disputes in which the eighteenth and nineteenth centuries delighted, while for their part the Scots were reluctant to give up such a nationalistic gem. There are still defenders of Macpherson's claims, just as there are still flat-earthers, but the general conclusion seems to be that even if they weren't translations from Ossian, Macpherson's poems have merit in their own right. At any rate, the controversy did Macpherson no harm. He held a succession of sinecures and government agencies, became a Member of Parliament, and built Balavil, where he died in 1796. Whatever the morality of his claims, *Fingal* and the other Ossian poems entitle Macpherson to be regarded as one of the fathers of the romantic movement in literature. He also helped to give a permanent colouring to the literary view of Scotland. The effect is pointed up by the reactions of travellers more than a century apart. Edward Burt found the Highlands straightforwardly horrid. Macaulay and Dickens found them *significantly* horrid.

We are now approaching Scotland's major tourist belt. A couple of miles up the road from Balavil, towards Kincraig, is the Highland Wildlife Park, opened in 1972. Wade's road ran through the eastern side of the park, but is now obscured by the new A9 and by the service roads to the park itself. It has to be said that the intention behind the Wildlife Park – to re-create a Highland environment as it might have been before so many species of fauna became extinct – was better than its execution. Of all the species on display, perhaps the most curious is the common tourist, who can be seen moving slowly across the landscape in his family saloon as if part of some huge funeral cortège.

But there is more to come. A few miles farther on is the monstrous development at Aviemore, 'Scotland's unique all year, all weather Highland holiday, conference, entertainment and leisure complex'. The original impetus at Aviemore was provided by skiing, following the use of the area for Commando training during the Second World War, but development has long since outpaced the requirements of this modest activity. 'With five T-bar tows in Coire Cas,' reports an early handout from the Highlands and Islands Development Board, '4500 skiers an hour can be whisked up to the high slopes. The middle station of the Chairlift links up with the White Lady Shieling, notable for the Doctor Who telephone kiosk plonked down outside the entrance. . . . Perched beside the top terminal is the Ptarmigan Observation Restaurant, an impudent pimple on the majestic brow of Cairngorm, and at 3650 feet indisputably the highest restaurant in Great Britain.' But skiing lasts, at best, four months, and so it has been necessary to bring in other attractions to keep the tills ringing: 'the unique Santa Claus Land, Highland Craft Village, Scotland's Clan Tartan Centre and shopping centres for holiday browsing … Britain's biggest all year ice rink, curling, squash, heated indoor leisure pool and swimming, saunas, solarium and paddling pool as well as a fitness gym.' All this, of course, makes Aviemore an easy target; but it would be less easy if one could be sure that the money generated there stayed in the Highlands, that the jobs went to local people, that the importation of such alien culture did not bring instability with it, and that as many tourists who might have been attracted by the area's natural merits, but are repelled by the new order, are replaced by those lured by the original (if not, by now, 'traditional') Doctor Who telephone kiosk and the impudent pimple on the majestic brow of Cairngorm.

However, the old A9, the new A9 and the tourist development have, between them, disposed of most traces of Wade at this point, and the next walkable stretch begins some five miles north, cutting across country to avoid the present road's detour to Carrbridge. After following the west side of the Spey valley, Wade's line turned sharply northwest beyond Kinveachy Lodge and struck out more or less in a direct line for the Slochd Pass. The walk begins opposite the junction of the A95 with the old A9 and leads westward across forestry land over Kinveachy Hill. After crossing a minor road from Carrbridge, it turns down through a grove of birch and juniper to Sluggan, an abandoned homestead used by sheep but still within reach of restoration. Sluggan Bridge itself is remarkably high, but although it is of some antiquity it is not the original Wade structure. This, which had two arches, was swept away in flood water.

From the bridge, the present path leads past a ruined croft (or possibly bridge house) on the right and then turns sharp left alongside a thin stream skirting a bracken-covered hillside, climbing

the opposite side of the valley after about 200 yards. Looking back from this point, however, the original Wade alignment can be seen leading forward from the end of the bridge across what is now a boggy patch. A secondary path leading eastwards from the ruin and disappearing among the trees is the remnant of a later military road which connected Sluggan Bridge with Carrbridge and, ultimately, Grantown. It can be walked for about three miles as far as the outskirts of Carrbridge, but care must be taken on the return, westward, journey to keep to the lower of the branching tracks about half a mile before Sluggan.

Returning to the Wade road, the path leads upwards from the bridge to where, at the top of the slope, are five mounded ruins, two of which have circular outlines. There is a strange 'lost garden' effect here, enhanced by more juniper trees. At the end of the juniper wood there is a moderately difficult section over boggy ground, and Wade's line has been lost. The best plan is to strike left to pick up the ruin of what was probably a sheepfold, and follow this until the Wade track emerges again from the right while, on the left, a view over the Dulnain opens up. Below, halfway between the path and the river, is Inverlaidnan House, in an older version of which, now in ruins, Prince Charles spent the night on his retreat to Culloden. Wade continued round the foot of Inverlaidnan Hill towards Slochd, taking the outermost of the rival tracks and skirting the forest except for one short stretch of a quarter of a mile or so. The track goes over the railway and alongside it to the right until it is lost under the new road near the Slochd summit.

It is a pity that the Wade road is so heavily overlaid at this point, for in Wade's day it was a spectacular piece of road engineering, 'at first', according to Edward Burt, 'thought to be insurmountable'. Visiting Slochd for the first time, Burt found it 'most horrible'. He wrote:

This is a deep, narrow hollow, into which huge parts of rocks have fallen. It is a terrifying sight to those who are not accustomed to such views; and at bottom is a small but dangerous burn, running wildly among the rocks, especially in times of rain. You descend by a declivity in the face of the mountain, from whence the rocks have parted (for they have visibly their decay), and the rivulet is particularly dangerous, when the passenger is going along with the stream, and pursued by the torrent. But you have not far to go in this bottom before you leave the current … and soon after you ascend by a steep and rocky hill, and when the height is attained, you would think the most rugged ways you could possibly conceive to be a happy variety.

Overcome by the experience, Burt, who was not normally free with money, gave his guide a shilling instead of the sixpence he had bargained for. 'Being told what it was, and that it was all his own, he fell on his knees and cried out', afterwards insisting on displaying to Burt his four almost naked children and praying with them for the English. All this led Burt into a long reflection on the theme that 'ruin is ruin, as much to the poor as to those that had been rich'.

The wild and terrifying spot that Burt described has been tamed by modern road-builders who, with the railway, have filled the narrow space available to the obliteration of everything else. But just after the summit the Wade line strikes to the right, as the right-hand track of a pair, to pass behind Creag an Tuim Bhig on its way to Raigbeg, emerging on the south side of the present bridge near the school. Raigbeg is a community apparently almost entirely given over to the bridging of the Findhorn. The railway crosses it by a splendid viaduct, the new A9 contributes a strictly functional prestressed concrete bridge, and the old road crosses the river by a more modest (though post-Wade) affair. From here on the Wade line is traceable on the map, but very much broken up on the ground, through Tomatin, Dalmagarry and Moy, until it emerges on the outskirts of Inverness as the Old Edinburgh Road.

If you have been following the story of the Forty-Five, you will want to take a diversion northeastwards to the site of Culloden, off the B9006 road about six miles from Inverness. Culloden has been written about extensively enough – some might say overwritten – to make a further account unnecessary here, but the visitor to the site should be warned to read up the battle beforehand. In contrast with its excellent visitor centres at Glencoe and Killiecrankie, the National Trust for Scotland has sadly failed its members at Culloden. Nor will understanding of the battle be greatly helped by the efforts of Duncan Forbes of Culloden House, in the late nineteenth century, to turn the battlefield into a kind of memorial garden. No doubt Duncan Forbes had authoritative sources to identify the grave mounds of the clan chiefs, but the effect of the crude headstones he caused to have erected – crude, it seems to me, in an effort to deceive – is to suggest that these were the actual graves marked shortly after the battle. Certainly the coachloads of visitors solemnly photograph the stones, thinking that they are taking pictures of history rather than what the Culloden site truly is, a reconstruction. Nearby, the 'Red Burn', said to have flowed scarlet with the blood of slain clansmen, suggests a touristic device to collect coins, as indeed it does. The cairn erected by Forbes, and in fact commemorating not the battle but his work of restoration on the site, is also much photographed. The whole scene, with its strong whiff of high toshery, does no service to Scottish history, but it has to be added that the disappointment of Culloden is not entirely Duncan Forbes's responsibility. The bleak moor of 1746 has, thanks to agricultural improvement, become luxuriant arable land, so that it is now impossible to imagine what it might have looked like when, shortly after one o'clock in the afternoon of 16 April 1746, the first Hanoverian cannon signalled the beginning of the end of Scotland's last rebellion.

6

Down the Great Glen

The pivot and starting point of General Wade's plan for control of the Highlands, spelt out in detail in his report of December 1724, was command of the Great Glen from Inverness to Fort William and rapid communication along it. Before the Wade roads were built, travellers to Scotland tended to go by sea, and it was from the sea that English interests in the Highlands were vulnerable to pro-Jacobite support forces from Flanders, Spain and Portugal. As Wade noted in his report, there had been a steady trade since 1715 in imported arms which had arrived in this way. The road down the Great Glen also gave Wade's men access to the wild lands of the west coast where, after the failure of the Fifteen, the clans had retreated into sullen plotting spiced with their traditional sport and occupation of cattle-stealing.

The rebuilding of Fort William, Fort George at Inverness and Kilcumein, renamed Fort Augustus, were put in hand within two years of Wade's arrival in Scotland. Wade's Fort George, on the site now occupied by Inverness Prison, is not to be confused with the present Fort George at Ardersier Point, twelve miles away. This, still in military use, was built after the Forty-Five, during which, in February 1746, Wade's Fort George was besieged by Prince Charles's troops, overcome and subsequently mined and completely destroyed. Wade's site had been occupied by a castle since the twelfth century, but in the seventeenth it had fallen into ruins. The foundation stone of the new fort, built to house up to six companies of soldiers, was laid in the summer of 1726.

There was already a barracks at Kilcumein, built after the Fifteen on what is now the site of the Lovat Arms Hotel. (A remnant can still be seen behind the hotel.) Wade judged this to be too far from Loch Ness, and so built a redoubt about half a mile away on the present site of the Benedictine abbey and school. The two military installations together, with 'communication made for their mutual support' could house an infantry battalion. Work on the new Fort

Augustus began in 1727 but was not finished until 1742. It was rendered uninhabitable only four years later when rebels occupied the older section and bombarded the newer, striking a direct hit on the powder magazine. It will have become clear that Wade's high hopes for the forts of the Great Glen were unjustified, and indeed, with two down and one to go, the Jacobites would almost certainly have taken Fort William if, while they were on their way there, they had not been called away to Culloden. They were greatly helped in their manoevrability by the road that the English had obligingly built through their territory.

Fort Augustus was rebuilt in 1747, and was visited by Dr Johnson in 1773, when he spent there 'the best night I have had these twenty years'. The military finally abandoned the fort in 1854, and in 1867 Lord Lovat acquired it for £5000, later presenting it, with some surrounding land, to the Benedictines. Little remains of the fort, and there is no telling whether those remnants there are belong to the 1747 building or to Wade's. Some of the walls of a fort (whichever one) are said to be incorporated in the present building, designed by Pugin and built in the 1880s, and looking towards Loch Ness from the swing bridge a watchtower can be seen commanding the entrance to the locks. Surprisingly, the Benedictine monks of Fort Augustus have their place in modern Scottish industrial history: in 1890 they built an 18-kilowatt hydroelectric plant, the first of its kind in Scotland and the precursor of many.

The third of Wade's Great Glen forts, Fort William, had been built in 1650, originally of turf and wattle and known as Inverlochy. (This was not the only alternative name in Fort William's history. The town has also been known at various times as Duncansburgh, Maryburgh and Gordonsburgh.) The fort had subsequently been strengthened and enlarged, and it successfully resisted Jacobite attack in the Fifteen. Of the three major forts of the Great Glen, Fort William's fate was perhaps the most ignominious. Abandoned by the military in 1855 and sold off, it eventually passed into the hands of the West Highland Railway Company. For a time the barracks were used by navvies, but when they had finished all except one room — the governor's room — was blown up, the entrance archway having been removed stone by stone to form the gateway to the town cemetery. The governor's room was preserved, however, with a caretaker to look after it, until the 1930s, when the panelling and

Benedictine abbey and school,
Fort Augustus

stairway leading to it were removed to the West Highland Museum in Fort William, where it can still be seen. The building itself was demolished, like the rest of the fort, and until the 1970s the fort site was occupied by Fort William railway station. Now, it is a car park.

As a temporary measure while the roads between the forts were being built, a galley was stationed on Loch Ness. This was, in General Wade's words, 'a small vessel with oars and sails, sufficient to carry a party of sixty or eighty soldiers and provisions for the garrison'. By 1725 he was able to report that the vessel had been completed and launched, and Edward Burt was on hand to record the occasion: 'When she made her first trip,' Burt wrote, 'she was mightily adorned with colours, and fired her guns several times, which was a strange sight to the Highlanders, who had never seen the like before, at least on that inland lake.' The firing of the guns attracted Highlanders from the hills, Burt added, 'lost in surprise and admiration'.

Despite a near disaster on one occasion when the galley almost ran aground on rocks with the General himself aboard, this curious craft   *Loch Lochy*

and its successors were maintained on Loch Ness until the early years of the nineteenth century, when it was pressed into service to transport materials for the building of the Caledonian Canal.

Having thus secured some measure of policing along the shores of Loch Ness, Wade made the road from Fort Augustus to Fort William his first priority. For the purposes of this book, however, we take the whole road, some sixty miles long, in one, starting from the northern end at Inverness.

Wade made two attempts on the Inverness to Fort Augustus route, and both of these, running more or less parallel, are attributed to him on the Ordnance Survey map. The earlier version, built in 1727 and 1728, took an inland route through Essich and across moorland to Torness. It was a forbidding route, blocked in winter, but it avoided the necessity for a difficult river crossing at Inverfarigaig (the bridge there cost £150 when Wade eventually built it in 1732) and for blasting a road surface out of solid rock. In 1732 Wade tried again, with a route which hugs the eastern shore of Loch Ness as far as Foyers and which involved some perilous navvy work, described by Edward Burt in a famous passage. 'There was no way at all along the edge of this lake till this part of the road was made,' Burt wrote. 'It is, good part of it, made out of rocks; but, among them all, I shall mention but one, which is of a great length, and, as I have said before, as hard as marble.' This was Black Rock, between Dores and Inverfarigaig.

There the miners hung by ropes from the precipice over the water (like Shakespeare's gatherers of samphire from Dover Cliffs) to bore the stone, in order to blow away a necessary part from the face of it, and the rest likewise was chiefly done by gunpowder; but when any part was fit to be left as it was, being flat and smooth, it was brought to a roughness proper for a stay to the feet; and in this part, and all the rest of the road, where the precipices were like to give horror or uneasiness to such as might pass over them in carriages, though at a good distance from them, they are secured to the lakeside by walls, either left in the working, or built up with stone, to a height proportioned to the occasion.

Even so, strong nerves were needed, as the intrepid Hon. Mrs Sarah Murray noted in her 1799 account of a journey along the Black Rock road:

In truth, it does require courage and steady horses to perform it, it being a narrow shelf blown out of the rocks; and to get upon it is by a road almost as steep as the ridge of a house, winding round a huge projecting mass, that looks as if it were ready to crush the bold adventurer who dares come under its brow; for it actually hangs over part of the carriage in passing it. … The scene made me amends for the little palpitation occasioned by the attainment of the awful eminence on which I was mounted.

Such excitements are not for the modern traveller, for subsequent road-widening has taken the terror out of the Black Rock and removed the opportunity for little palpitations. On the lochside, however, there is the contemporary *frisson* of looking for the Loch Ness monster, and indeed almost anything seems possible in these deep and brooding waters. Until the early 1930s, when Scotland began to be opened up to the touring motorist in a fairly determined fashion, the B852 – Wade's lochside road – was the main route to Inverness. Then the road on the west side, through Drumnadrochit, was built, and in July 1933, to the continuing joy of the Scottish tourist industry, a Mr and Mrs Spicer, driving along the new road, saw something crossing in front of them. They stopped and watched as the 'abomination' disappeared from view. 'It was like a huge snail with a long neck,' Mr Spicer reported later.

The Spicers had no camera with them, but within a year two photographs of the monster had been taken, the first of many. A new industry had been born. Medieval manuscripts were found to contain what might (or on the other hand might not) be taken as references to a Loch Ness monster. Local folklore was said to abound in tales of such a creature. No one, at the time, thought it curious that although Loch Ness had been a magnet for tourists, on purely scenic grounds, for at least a century and a half, none of these travellers, many of whom wrote detailed accounts of their journeys, apparently either saw the monster themselves or heard stories about it. Meanwhile, tourist authorities in adjacent areas searched their own lochs closely in case they, too, should prove to contain shadows which, in suitable lights, might be monsters. But this was in vain. Loch Ness had the head start, and popular science, popular para-psychology, mass hysteria, television rights, and the willingness of people to believe anything have now brought the matter to the point where there is a whole visitor centre devoted to the monster and the array of modern technology which has been brought to bear on the question. New pictures, some clearly of tree trunks, continue to appear from time to time, and it is as if the art of photographic

The entrance to Loch Ness, Fort Augustus

retouching had never been heard of. But gullibility is not the prerogative of simple folk; one of the first grants to aid tourism made by the Highlands and Islands Development Board in the 1960s was a payment of £1000 to assist in the hunt for the monster, a gesture greeted by Scotsmen, according to Magnus Magnusson, 'without amusement or enthusiasm'. Actually, if you want to see a monster in Loch Ness, you can see half a dozen in half an hour by simply watching the water, if you are at all suggestible.

Most of the holiday traffic to Inverness is on the A82 on the northwest side of Loch Ness, leaving the Wade road relatively quiet and so walkable, except for a tedious slog through two miles of Inverness suburbs. Both the 1727 and the 1732 roads leave Inverness by the B862, but the earlier, inland, route forks left through Drummond, heading for Essich. It is a pleasant though exposed walk, best done in good weather with a light wind, along minor roads which occasionally become mere tracks, as for about two miles at the southern end of Loch Ashie. The B862 is then rejoined to take you through a fairly narrow pass alongside Loch Ceo Glais to Torness. About one mile beyond Eudinuagain, the Wade line strikes to the right, higher than the B862, following farm tracks for about two miles before rejoining the road at Newlands, a mile or so from

Errogie. From here on, the route is a mystery, and there is scope for some original Wade-hunting if you have the taste for it. According to J. B. Salmond, writing in 1934 and basing his account on a manuscript map of 1730 in Inverness Public Library, the 1727 road 'crossed the present Inverfarigaig–Errogie road about a mile north of Errogie and continued by Lochgarthside to the ford over Gourag where Wade broke off to go down by Foyers with his 1732 road.' Read against the Ordnance Survey map, this makes no sense. The Inverfarigaig–Errogie road runs almost due west to east, so there can be no crossing a mile north of Errogie. Furthermore, the Ordnance Survey shows Wade's earlier road quite distinctly rejoining the B862 at Newlands, and there is no possible alternative (either on the map or on the ground) at this point. It seems likely that from the junction Wade followed the line of the present road, heading towards Whitebridge and joining the 1732 alignment, as Salmond said, at the River Foyers crossing. There are some suggestive tracks through the woodland between Errogie and Loch Ness, and another along the west side of the Fechlin ending at Whitebridge, but experienced Wade-followers will have learned not to take too much notice of hazy evidence like this. Salmond admits that he did not trace his proposed route on the ground, and I suspect that the answer to the puzzle lies in the imperfections of the eighteenth-century map which he quotes as his source. In any case, considering the amount of agricultural improvement and forestry work in this area, together with the fact that Wade's inland route was in use for only five years, it would be surprising if his line could be traced intact today.

The lochside road, substantially along the line of the B852, is an easier matter, though it too has its mystery: the exact location of the 'General's Hut' frequently referred to by successive writers of the eighteenth and nineteenth centuries. Johnson noted that he stayed at the General's Hut near Foyers on his 1773 journey to the Western Isles ('we found it not ill-stocked with provisions') and Boswell, in his account of the same tour, gives more details: 'We came to dinner to a public house called the General's hut. Near it is the meanest parish kirk I ever saw. It is a shame it should be on a high road. We had mutton-chops, a broiled chicken, and bacon and eggs, and a bottle of Malaga.' Leyden, travelling this way in 1800, stayed at the hut ('a wretched inn'), which he places on the Inverness side of the

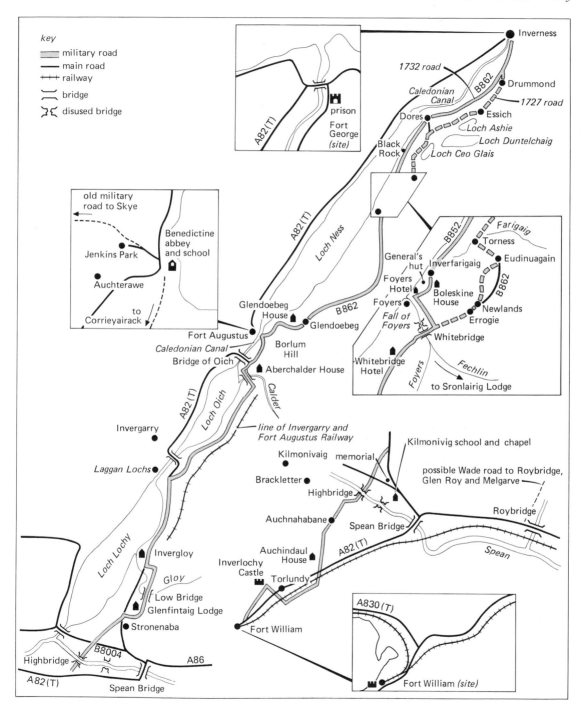

key
military road
main road
+++ railway
bridge
disused bridge

Inverness

1732 road
B862
Drummond
Caledonian Canal
1727 road
Dores
Essich
Loch Ashie
Black Rock
Loch Duntelchaig
Loch Ceo Glais

prison
Fort George *(site)*
A82 (T)

old military road to Skye
Jenkins Park
Benedictine abbey and school
Auchterawe
to Corrieyairack

A82 (T)
Loch Ness

B852
Farigaig
Torness
General's hut
Inverfarigaig
Eudinuagain
Foyers Hotel
Boleskine House
Foyers
Newlands
B862
Glendoebeg House
B862
Glendoebeg
Fall of Foyers
Errogie
Whitebridge
Fort Augustus
Caledonian Canal
Borlum Hill
Foyers
Whitebridge Hotel
Bridge of Oich
Aberchalder House
Fechlin
to Sronlairig Lodge

A82 (T)
Loch Oich
Calder
Invergarry
line of Invergarry and Fort Augustus Railway
Kilmonivaig school and chapel
Kilmonivaig
memorial
possible Wade road to Roybridge, Glen Roy and Melgarve
Brackletter
Highbridge
Roybridge
Laggan Lochs
Auchnahabane
Spean Bridge
Loch Lochy
Auchindaul House
A82 (T)
Spean
Invergloy
Gloy
Inverlochy Castle
Low Bridge
Torlundy
Glenfintaig Lodge
Stronenaba
Fort William
Highbridge
B8004
A86
A82 (T)
Spean Bridge

A830 (T)
Fort William *(site)*

Fall of Foyers. Southey, in 1819, gives a further description: 'Boleskin, better known by the name of the General's Hut ... built of mud and straw, within squares of wooden framing.' Southey says that the inn's visitors' book, reputed to have been kept up since Wade's time, was 'stolen by some scoundrel a few years ago'.

Clearly, if the General's Hut was indeed the building that Southey described it would not have survived for very long and is unlikely to have been the original. However, it has been suggested that Southey's inn was not the actual 'hut' but built on or near its site. Wade's own map of the King's Roads, dated 1746, places the hut a little more than a mile south of Inverfarigaig, the site of a Wade bridge. There is, at this point, a ruined chapel and a graveyard, built between road and loch in the Gaelic manner, opposite Boleskine House. This would seem to fit both Southey's and Boswell's locations and, suggestively, a path runs from the loch side of the graveyard to the grounds of Foyers Hotel, said by some others to be the site of the original hut. It may be that over the years the licence changed hands and locations, and the name of the inn moved with it. However that

Near Foyers

may be, the churchyard (despite Boswell, the chapel is not Boleskine parish kirk, which is two miles away towards Whitebridge, near the junction of the two Wade roads) is worth a visit. The chapel is long since roofless and abandoned, but the gravestones provide an outline social history of this area going back over three hundred years.

Foyers itself was the site, now unhappily closed, of one of the most hopeful industrial projects to be started in the Highlands, and one of the earliest. In 1894 the North British (later British) Aluminium Company, looking for a source of cheap and reliable electricity for the aluminium reduction process, bought the Foyers estate and began to build Britain's first sizeable hydroelectric scheme. Its output was over two hundred times that of the monks' small plant at Fort Augustus, built only four years before, and this is an indication of the pace at which development in this field was moving, despite the fact that it was inhibited at this time by the lack of power transmission technology and electricity had to be consumed where it was produced. Hydro power and aluminium reduction are among the least offensive trappings of industry, and it is a pity that, having established a lead for Scotland in both a new style of power generation and a new metal industry, Foyers could not retain it. All went well in the early years, with the Foyers plant producing, at one stage, one sixth of the world supply of pure aluminium. It could not have come to an area more desperately in need of employment. Sadly, Foyers paid the penalty of pioneering success. The new material found an ever-increasing market, and to satisfy this bigger and better plants were built, not only in Scotland at Kinlochleven, but also in Scandinavia and Canada. The Foyers contribution as a proportion of the whole dwindled until, in the 1960s, the plant closed. It was one of many disappointments faced by those who have tried to take Scotland's industry out of its heavy engineering and steelfounding traditions into newer fields.

Shortly after the junction of the two Wade roads beyond Foyers, you come to Whitebridge. The old bridge, beside the present one, is genuine Wade, engineered in 1732 by William Caulfield and probably replacing an earlier timber structure. A few yards farther on is the Whitebridge Hotel, built on the site of a former kingshouse. The walk to Sronlairig Lodge by Loch Killin, suggested in Chapter 3 as part of a possible military route to Inverness, begins by the bridge and is clearly signposted.

Whitebridge

Then follows a splendid march down to Fort Augustus along a road that, though widened for tourist traffic, is pleasantly walkable and follows the Wade line as far as Glendoebeg. Here, Wade forked right, rejoining the present road just below Glendoebeg House. At the foot of Borlum Hill he took another right fork, skirting the woods for about half a mile before descending steeply with the present road to Fort Augustus.

I am going to suggest that at Fort Augustus you leave Wade's Great Glen road behind for a while and sample part of what is left of an older military road, the old road to Skye. Up to a few years ago there was more to be walked, but road improvements and a hydroelectric scheme in Glen Moriston have either overlaid or flooded tracks which were until relatively recently walkable as far as the inn at Cluanie. The road led on through Kintail, past Shiel Bridge to Glenelg, the crossing point for Skye.

Its early history is unclear, but the route was used by drovers and

Opposite: *Wade's bridge,*
Whitebridge

Glen Moriston

there must have been at least a track through Glen Moriston and
Glen Shiel to reach Bernera Barracks, near Glenelg, which were built
about 1720. Wade was not impressed with the siting of Bernera, and
perhaps for this reason the Glenelg road was not among his priorities.
It was his successor, William Caulfield, who engineered the road in
1755, and Telford's commissioners remade it in the 1820s. Although
the major tourist route for Skye is now via Mallaig from Fort
William, the older road still attracts enough traffic in the season to
deter the walker, but the few miles off the road give unparalleled
views of the Great Glen, the Corrieyairack, Kintail and the mountains
of Skye.

The road starts at the northern end of Fort Augustus, turning
away from Loch Ness at Brae House and following the signposts for
Auchterawe and Jenkins Park. After about half a mile the road takes
a sharp left turn, but the military road goes straight on past some
bungalows until it peters out to a track marked with a Scottish
Rights of Way Society sign. There follows a steepish climb up a set

of zigzags reminiscent of, but by no means as punishing as, those on the Corrieyairack road, and then through Inchnacardoch Forest to the 1250-foot contour, which the track follows for about a mile. Once off the ridge, it turns to the west with a tricky crossing of the Allt Phocaichain, skirts Ceannacroc Forest and then plunges into it for the last mile or so, meeting the new road at Achlain. This is one of those walks that present a different, and equally spectacular, aspect in each direction, and it makes a pleasant and not too demanding day out – perhaps for a walker who needs to recover after the Corrieyairack.

Boswell and Johnson between them left a very good account of this road as it was in 1773 when they journeyed along it to Skye. It was at an inn (now vanished) at Ceannacroc village, about four miles west of Achlain, that Johnson gave the party of soldiers they had met earlier 'two shillings to drink', with the consequences described in Chapter 2. Boswell was much taken with the landlord's daughter – 'a modest civil girl very neatly dressed' – who served them tea, and Johnson gave her a book of arithmetic which he happened to have about him. But Boswell worried about bugs in the bed and was glad to leave. Worse lay ahead at the inn at Glenelg: a 'raw and dirty' room with a wretched bed; little to eat in the house; nothing to drink but whisky. Boswell studied the barracks and envied the garrison. Scotland made few concessions to travellers in those days.

Returning to Fort Augustus and the Great Glen road, the junction of Wade's two roads leading respectively on to Fort William and over the Corrieyairack has now been lost, as noted in Chapter 3, perhaps as the result of river changes when the Caledonian Canal was built. The Fort Augustus to Fort William stretch is in any case not suitable for walking, since it carries all the traffic bound for Loch Ness and Inverness, and south of Invergarry much of that bound by way of Kyle to Skye and Wester Ross – a route greatly favoured by caravaners. Where the new road deviates from Wade the original line has either been lost or is now inaccessible.

At Bridge of Oich, where the A82 turns right, crosses the canal and heads for Invergarry, Wade kept to the south side of the loch, turning away to bridge the Calder just past Aberchalder House. Here, for about five miles, two abandoned means of transport run together: Wade's road by the lochside and, on its left, the short-lived and derelict Invergarry and Fort Augustus Railway. This quite

Invergarry Castle

hopeless enterprise, one of the last flings of railway mania, connected at Spean Bridge with the West Highland line. It was completed in 1898, though owing to legal wrangles it was not until 1903 that the first trains ran. The line was uneconomic from the start – its annual takings from passengers and goods together rarely topped £1000 – and for two years, from 1911 to 1913, it was closed down. Opened again in time for what traffic could be gleaned from wartime, it lingered on afterwards as a passenger line until 1933, and from then on until 1946 for a weekly coal train. Then the rails were lifted.

Edward Burt gives a hair-raising account of the old way along

Glen Garry and Loch Oich

Loch Oich before Wade's men arrived. 'The rocks,' he said, 'project over the lake, and the path was so rugged and narrow that the Highlanders were obliged, for their safety, to hold by the rocks and shrubs as they passed, with the prospect of death beneath them.' To make this rough way plain 'required a great quantity of gunpowder'; but, Burt claims, the end result was a road 'as commodious as any other of the roads in the Highlands, which everywhere (bating ups and downs) are equal in goodness to the best in England.' Opinions may differ about that, but the track can be followed, obscured from time to time by the old railway line, until the Wade road rejoins the

A82 at Laggan Locks after running through a settlement of holiday chalets whose tenants would no doubt be amazed to hear that their quarters are built across one of Scotland's oldest roads. Old and new roads run together as far as Invergloy, where Wade turned away from the loch to cross the River Gloy at Low Bridge, in the grounds of Glenfintaig Lodge, rejoining the present road just beyond the Lodge itself.

There is little to detain the Wade-hunter between here and Highbridge, which is approached along Wade's track leading away from the A82 to the right at Stronenaba. Crossing the B8004, Wade headed for the Spean and ran alongside the river on the approach to the bridge. This was one of Wade's grander efforts, with three arches, and the laying of its foundation stone in June 1736 was celebrated with many loyal toasts – it was also the anniversary of George II's accession – and the firing of guns, and later that day, in Fort William, more toasts, 'bonfires, illuminations and all other demonstrations of joy'. But Highbridge is a sad sight now, with only

Wade's road above Loch Lochy

the ruin of its fifty-foot central arch remaining. A mile or so upstream, and visible as you approach from the north, is another abandoned bridge which carried the Invergarry and Fort Augustus Railway across the Spean. This, as if to compete with Wade, was also on the grand scale: four lattice spans carried on piers seventy-six feet high. Today, only the piers remain.

Highbridge was where the very first engagement of the Forty-Five took place. Characteristically for a campaign whose main events on both sides were dictated by chance rather than design, the first meeting of Jacobite and Hanoverian was an accident. Prince Charles had first set foot on Scottish soil on 23 July 1745, on Eriskay. Moving on to Arisaig, he received promises of support from the Macdonalds of Keppoch and Glencoe and from the Camerons of Lochiel, all of whom had been identified in General Wade's report of 1724 as among 'the clans most addicted to rapine and plunder'. They had also been among the leading offenders under the Disarming Act and had good weapons concealed in the turf roofs of their homes.

Beside Loch Lochy

Wade's bridge at Highbridge

English intelligence seems to have been slow, or to have underrated the strength of the Prince's following. The forts along the Great Glen were only lightly garrisoned, and it was not until 10 August that two small companies under the command of Captain Scott and Captain Thomson set out from Perth, by way of the Corrieyairack, for Fort William. This was the advance party of a much larger force that Cope was assembling at Stirling, and which eventually set out on 20 August. Meanwhile, as described in Chapter 3, preparations were being made, rather saucily, for the raising of Prince Charles's standard at Glenfinnan.

The two English captains and their men, after halting at Fort Augustus, reached Highbridge to discover that it was already occupied by a party of Macdonalds. In fact, there were only about a dozen of them, but Donald Macdonald, their leader, had instructed them to move about among the boulders and trees, showing themselves at intervals, to give the impression of a larger force. Visitors to Highbridge can readily understand the reluctance of the King's troops to run the risk of an ambush in this confined spot, and a sergeant and one man were sent forward to try and establish the strength of the enemy. They literally walked into the Macdonalds' arms.

The remainder of the party retreated hastily under fire, going back the way they had come and evidently making for Fort Augustus. But their nerve had been badly shaken — most of the party were newly enlisted men and already exhausted by the long march from Perth — and Captain Scott decided to seek refuge at Invergarry Castle. This was a mistake, since Glengarry of Invergarry had already pledged himself to Prince Charles and assembled a force at the castle for the gathering at Glenfinnan. His force now opened fire on Scott's party, killing a sergeant and four others and wounding Scott himself. The King's troops were obliged to surrender, Captain Scott being allowed to proceed to Fort William with an escort of the enemy, to have his wounds attended to. It was an ignominious start.

There is an opportunity in the Highbridge area for some detective work which could help to solve a mystery raised by at least two Wade experts, A. R. B. Haldane and J. B. Salmond. Both think it possible that Wade made a road eastward from Highbridge up Glen Roy to join the Corrieyairack road at Melgarve, though there is no mention of it in Wade's records. What is certain is that Roybridge

and Melgarve are linked today by, in succession, a metalled road for about ten miles, a Land Rover track, and finally a footpath. This route is shown on a map of 1725, and also on the military map produced by General Roy in 1755, after Wade. There would have been some strategic sense in building the route into the military network, since in the absence in those days of the Loch Laggan road, communication between Ruthven and Fort William was roundabout and time-consuming. In Wade's terms, for he was not greatly disturbed by boggy ground and so would not have found the Melgarve end of the route too daunting, the prospect of a southern link between the two great north–south routes must have been tempting. However, neither Haldane nor Salmond, after extensive researches, could find confirmation that such a road was ever built, though both suspected it. On the ground there is at least a suspicion that they were right.

The road, if it had been built, would no doubt have joined the Great Glen road near Highbridge, on the north side to avoid a

Near Highbridge, downstream from Spean Bridge

second crossing of the Spean. Our researches begin at the turning off the A82 to Kilmonivaig church and school, about half a mile northwest of Spean Bridge. Opposite the church is a stile which leads immediately into a sea of bog cotton. After about thirty yards of squelchy walking parallel to the school playground, a track becomes visible, leading westwards and rising slightly. Though badly decayed, there are traces of a former road surface and of the characteristic military bank and ditch formation. The track is traceable to the right as far as the approach to Highbridge, and on its right is a banked enclosure, possibly the remains of some kind of encampment.

My suspicions about this track were boosted when I came across a dowser picking his way downhill from the direction of the Second World War monument, rods in hand. He was spending his retirement, he said, looking for 'Bonnie Prince Charlie's treasure' – the bullion supposed to have been provided by the French and Portuguese to support the Forty-Five but left behind in the final debacle. (Also on the trail of this considerable treasure, the dowser told me, was the Duke of Argyll.) The trail led across the stile, over the road and into the churchyard, where the dowser was reluctant to be seen with his divining rods. All the same, this seemed to suggest something, if only that the track was real enough. As to whether it is a Wade route or not, this cannot be answered until someone rediscovers another original map of Wade's work.

South of Highbridge, Wade went southwest to a point where the minor metalled road to Brackletter makes a right-angled turn, and his line can be seen heading straight on towards Auchnahabane. About two miles beyond, he bore left towards the present main road, crossing it at the lane leading to Auchindaul. House, and so under the railway. From here on into Fort William his line appears only intermittently on the right-hand side of the road as far as the road junction near Torlundy, where it becomes the drive to Inverlochy Castle, passes the castle and rejoins the A82 just short of the point where road and river meet.

The Hon. Mrs Sarah Murray, travelling this way in 1799, reported that the journey from Spean Bridge to Fort William was 'the most dreary, though not the ugliest, space I had travelled in Scotland', inhabited by 'the poorest of the poor' whose mean huts could hardly be distinguished from the moor, so dense was the vegetation that grew on their turf roofs. Times have changed. The most notable features of this road today are the stations of the Great Glen Cattle Ranch, a beef production enterprise started in 1944 which has transformed the Lochy valley.

Fort William gave the impression, until recently, of an honest, though a little down-at-heel, working town, with the tourist element unobtrusive except along the road to the south. The businesslike atmosphere was largely due, I think, to the uncompromising presence at the west end of the main street, between the town and the loch, of the West Highland Railway station, sidings and engine sheds. No doubt the burghers of Fort William felt that this made an insufficiently impressive entrance to the town for tourists. In 1975 the railway track was shortened by a few hundred yards and a new station was opened at the east end of the town, with the engine sheds banished outside the town altogether. The old station, which was on the site of the fort, smelt of fish and trade. The new one is unmistakably a tourist terminus, with a tourist office incorporated into the building. Though perhaps there is local dissent: on a signpost pointing to 'Tourist information' someone, when I was there last, had aerosolled 'Go home'. The improvements at the station end of Fort William's main street present the familiar picture of planning for planning's sake. In place of an attractive old row of shops is a new shopping precinct, with the usual story of leases not taken up because rents are too high and so going eventually to organizations to whom outgoings are less critical – the Job Centre, the Department of Health and Social Security and the District Council. Behind this, the area formerly occupied by railway track has been given over to car parking, of which a large proportion is taken up by reserved bays, protected by lockable pillars, no doubt for the exclusive use of the bureaucrats. In the closing stages of the Forty-Five, Fort William managed to hold out. Against the planners, though, it seems there can be no resistance.

7

Walking Through Lochaber

The temptation to include in this book part of the military road from Fort William southwards to Stirling is irresistible, for all that it was not given military status until after Wade's time. It runs through country as remote as the Corrieyairack, skirting the wilds of Rannoch Moor, climbing to over 1800 feet over the Devil's Staircase, and taking in the sombre memories of Glencoe. And yet a good part of it, almost incredibly, was until the 1930s the main road from the south.

If any further justification is needed, this walk, or any part of it, would fit in well to a walking tour of the Highlands, taking you back from Fort William towards Aberfeldy by way of Loch Tay road or, alternatively, back to Glasgow by rail. As the newly designated West Highland Way, the Fort William to Tyndrum section described here can be followed by farm roads, disused railway lines and estate roads – all amply indicated by 'thistle' markers – as far as Milngavie on the northwestern outskirts of Glasgow.

The military alignment from Fort William to Stirling by way of Crianlarich, Lochearnhead and Callander was made between 1748 and 1752 by Wade's successor, William Caulfield, but the route had been already well established by that time as a drove road. The mountainous section from Fort William to Glencoe had been used in 1692, the year of the Glencoe massacre, by the enforcing troops. This section remained in military use for only about forty years after Caulfield built it, being replaced by the existing road through Glencoe village and then round the shores of Loch Linnhe. Though considerably longer, the later route avoided the punishing climb up the Devil's Staircase and almost equally demanding pulls in and out of Kinlochleven.

Since 1980 this road has formed part of the West Highland Way. Many lovers of this area – including me – held their breath when this plan was announced, fearing the municipalization of what is essentially a wild walk. We need not have worried. The waymarks are unobtrusive, there have been no 'improvements' beyond a little clearance here and there, and the policy seems to be that once walkers have had their attention directed to the route they are left to get on with it. The way was already (at least from Crianlarich northwards) well known to serious walkers, and since it was made official there seems to have been little noticeable increase in traffic, probably because each leg is long and demanding enough to deter casual ramblers.

The West Highland Way leaves Fort William by way of Glen Nevis along a road which, in season, is as congested as Piccadilly Circus. This was presumably to give the walk added tourist appeal, but it was not the way taken by Caulfield. He left the town to the south. From the car park at the southern end of the town centre, fork left from the coast road through a distressing area of peeling council houses which, fortunately, ends suddenly at a cattle grid and leads directly onto open moorland. The road is now quiet, winding and dipping past the tiny settlement of Blarmachfoldach and leading

Blàr a' Chaorainn

Loch Leven

on towards Lundavra Farm, a distance of about six miles from Fort William. Do not be led astray by the farm road, however; Caulfield's line leaves the road beside a derelict cottage, Blàr a' Chaorainn, and continues due south on the opposite side of the glen from Lundavra. The way ahead now is clearly marked by electricity pylons, which follow the military road all the way to Kinlochleven. The track coming in from the right at Lairigmór cottage leads to Callert on Loch Leven, opposite Glencoe village, where there was once a regular ferry service which saved a ten-mile diversion through Kinlochleven. From Lairigmór, the military road gradually veers southeast towards Kinlochleven, with a steepish zigzag descent just above the town.

Kinlochleven was the second stage, after Foyers, in the activities of the North British Aluminium Company, referred to in Chapter 6. Before 1904, it hardly existed as an identifiable community. In that year, the Aluminium Company began work on an ambitious project which included the building of the Blackwater Dam, almost half a mile long and 85 feet high, whose reservoir was to provide power for an aluminium reduction factory at Kinlochleven which, by 1909, was producing one third of the world's output. By all accounts, the navvies who came into the area for this work – there was, of course,

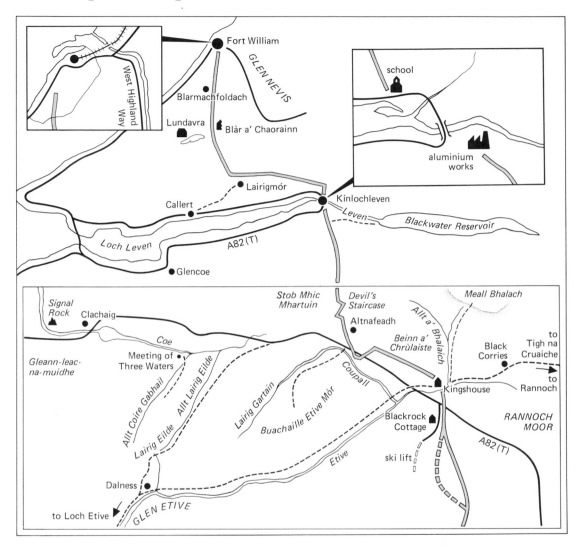

no local workforce available – gave Kinlochleven a lively early history. 'It was an incredible place of saloons and gambling dens,' says one report, 'where men flocked to work like gold prospectors of old. There were no policemen in Kinlochleven, except the two who came to escort the postman on his once-weekly round.'

The road from Fort William enters Kinlochleven (which apparently only narrowly escaped being called Aluminiumville) opposite

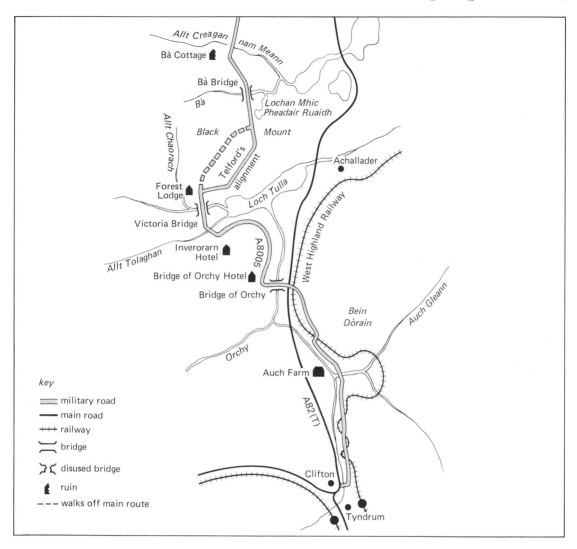

the school, and you have to cross the town to pick up the next leg to Glencoe. The way begins past the aluminium works, and for the first mile or so is made up. As you climb, the great sheet of Blackwater Reservoir comes into view ahead, with a track leading to the dam. Continue to bear right, however, for the military road which climbs round the shoulder of the north side of the Glencoe range in a series of winds and zigzags. It feels, and is, very exposed here, and one can imagine the feelings of the troops on this road, poised between the rigours of the climb from Kinlochleven and the unknown hostilities of Glencoe. The road now runs due south, with a stream to be forded beside an abandoned bothy or perhaps patrol post. It can be slow and sticky going here, with the added diversion of seeing some of what must surely be the largest slugs in Britain. A sharp pull across the shoulder of Stob Mhic Mhartuin brings you to the top of the Devil's Staircase and your first sight of Glencoe itself. This was the way taken on 1 February 1692 by the 120-strong force of Campbell troops who had come to destroy the Macdonalds of Glencoe. In the snow-covered glen before them MacIain, chief of the Macdonalds, and some forty of his kinsmen had only twelve days to live. The Campbells' mission was explicitly enough spelt out in their orders: 'To fall upon the rebels, the Macdonalds of Glencoe, and put all to the sword under seventy. You are to have a special care that the old fox and his sons do upon no account escape your hands. You are to secure all the avenues that no man escape.'

It was shortly before five in the morning of 13 February that a party of soldiers, with a lieutenant in charge, came to MacIain's house. The chief got up to greet them, and was shot in the back. His wife was stripped and beaten so severely that she died the next day. Two others in the house were killed and a third left for dead. The massacre had begun, and it went on throughout the day. Men, women and children who were caught were casually butchered. Homes were set on fire. Cattle were driven loose. Under cover of a blizzard, some of the people of Glencoe escaped into the hills, but whether they were able to survive in the bitter weather is not known.

It is a savage story, lightened only by a number of legends which suggest that some, at least, of the troops tried to warn the Macdonalds by playing a particular tune, that individual soldiers billeted in the cottages tried obliquely – too obliquely, it seems – to warn their hosts. I particularly like the story of the ex-soldier who, many years later, sought shelter for the night at a cottage in the glen. He was admitted reluctantly, and the welcome chilled even further when he confessed after supper that he had been in Glencoe in 1693. He told how his lieutenant had ordered him to kill a young boy and insisted on seeing the blood on the soldier's sword. To satisfy him, the soldier cut off the tip of the boy's finger, and emerged to wipe his

Aluminium works,
Kinlochleven

sword on the snow in front of his officer. When he finished his story, his Highland host and his wife were silent. Then the crofter called for more whisky, holding up his hand – with the tip of one finger missing.

It is hardly surprising that, as the background of this savage spurt of history, Glencoe should have attracted a reputation for gloom. Dickens, passing through in 1841, found it 'an awful place. There are scores of glens high up, which form such haunts as you might imagine yourself wandering in in the very height and madness of a fever. . . . The very recollection of them makes me shudder.' 'In the Gaelic tongue Glencoe signifies the Glen of Weeping,' confided Macaulay. In fact, it signifies nothing of the sort, and Macaulay was simply spreading it thick, as he was wont to do. Taking up another trowelful, he went on: 'In truth, that pass is the most dreary and melancholy of all the Scottish passes, the very Valley of the Shadow of Death. Mists and storms brood over it through the greater part of the finest summer; and even on those rare days when the sun is bright, and when there is no cloud in the sky, the impression made by the landscape is sad and awful.' Against this, it is worth recording that Dorothy Wordsworth, who might have been expected to react similarly (and admitted that she was ready to do so), found the glen 'open to the eye, the mountains retiring in independent majesty' when she visited it on a 'delightful' afternoon in 1803. But despite what Macaulay had to say, Glencoe doesn't make a great parade of its sad history, unlike Culloden. Curiously, two of the 'official' relics of the massacre both have clouds of doubt hanging over them. Signal Rock near Clachaig, said to be the spot from which the signal for the massacre was given, is thought to be an invention of the speculative school of nineteenth-century antiquarianism, and the supposed house where MacIain was slain, above Clachaig in Gleann-leac-na-muidhe, is, despite a commemorative stone, now thought to be misplaced. However, there are good, reliable accounts of the massacre at the visitor centre at Clachaig, and the tiny folk museum in Glencoe village is also worth a visit.

The Devil's Staircase brings the military road down beside a keeper's house at Altnafeadh, crosses the main road behind the Scottish Mountaineering Club house (formerly a crofter's cottage) and then turns alongside the A82 on the south side. After about a mile it recrosses the road and continues through a sheepfank and

Altnafeadh, looking west

under the electricity pylons beside the ruins of several cottages. This is a boggy stretch, and at the eastern end, where the military alignment joins the tarmac byroad to Kingshouse, the way is completely lost.

Kingshouse is one of a number of well-placed hotels which make this walk easy to do in some comfort and style. It claims (though it is by no means alone in this) to be the oldest inn in Scotland, and it has certainly been an inn for some 200 years, having earlier been a garrison post. It has had a bad press in the past. One traveller in 1818 noted with regret that it was impossible to avoid an overnight stop there, and in 1894 Murray's *Handbook* found Kingshouse only 'tolerable'. But the inn's most dissatisfied guest must have been Dorothy Wordsworth, who devoted two whole pages of her account of her 1803 journey to the iniquities of the place. The Wordsworths, accompanied by the ailing Coleridge, were met by a harridan 'screaming in Erse' who could hardly spare time to show them their

rooms. The place was 'as dirty as a house after a sale on a rainy day' and it was furnished so barely that it looked 'as if more than half the goods had been sold out'. It took a couple of hours to persuade the woman to light the fire, and supper consisted of 'a shoulder of mutton so hard that it was impossible to chew the little flesh that might be scraped off the bones, and some sorry soup made of barley and water, for it had no other taste.' The bed sheets were soaking wet and had to be dried by the poor fire before the guests could go to bed.

Altnafeadh, looking east towards Rannoch

It is time to redress the balance. Visitors to Kingshouse today will find (in season; the hotel is closed from November to February inclusive) an exceptionally comfortable place with excellent drying rooms, so that it is possible to indulge in that most delightful of walking experiences – arriving stiff and wet, stacking one's clothes to dry, changing after a bath and eating dinner in civilized comfort. You might well be tempted to stay on, in which case there are a number of good walks and simple scrambles to be explored in the area.

To the north of Kingshouse, a strenuous walk, with occasional scrambling, takes you up the Allt a' Bhalaich to the ridge of Meall Bhalach, from where you get a superb view across the Blackwater Reservoir towards Ben Nevis and beyond. Leaving the Kingshouse road at the junction with the path to Rannoch, which is signposted, take the east bank of the stream, crossing over to the west just before the pylons cross, after about one mile. There is no path, but the sheep tracks are adequate, and for long distances in the summer you can walk comfortably on the rocks of the stream bed. At the top, where the land opens out into a broad corrie, bear right for the ridge in order to avoid boggy ground. After admiring the view from the top, you can either return the same way or work your way round the north side of Beinn a' Chrùlaiste and go down the valley to Altnafeadh, and so back to Kingshouse along the military road.

The walk to Rannoch by way of Black Corries along the signposted path from Kingshouse is not recommended unless you have plenty of time, a compass, a watch and a good sense of direction, and should on no account be attempted except in the best of weather. As the water on the moor is unsafe to drink (even the railway cottages have their supplies brought in by rail) you must have your own supply with you. These warnings may sound extreme, but in fact it is all too easy to become disorientated on the moor, and there is absolutely no chance of finding anyone to ask the way. It is said that once, when a police search party combed the moor for a missing person, no less than four skeletons were found.

The walk – if you are still game – starts well enough along a cinder track as far as Black Corries, and along a lesser track for about three miles beyond; but then the way suddenly disintegrates. From here the track follows the power lines, with only slight deviations, but this makes it sound easier than it is. However, if you persist you will pass the ruined cottage of Tigh na Cruaiche and shortly afterwards find yourself on the shores of Loch Laidon. From here, it is about three miles to Rannoch station on the West Highland Railway. If you time it right (which is not easy, because there are only a handful of trains each day, and none on Sundays) you could take the train here for Bridge of Orchy, from where (again, with

*Kingshouse, Glencoe, and
Buachaille Etive Mór*

careful timing) you can take a bus back to the Kingshouse turning off the A82, or thumb a lift.

For a walk without these problems of timing, Glen Etive makes a good round trip. The road down the glen is made up, but it is quiet. It follows the Etive all the way to the head of Loch Etive, where the road stops at a pierhead. This was once the normal route to Glencoe, by sea from Taynuilt near Oban, and it was the way the Wordsworths came in 1803. No doubt the existence of this now forgotten route accounts for the well-engineered road, which seems almost too grand for its current usage. Return by the road through Dalness and then, on a sharp bend just north of Dalness itself, follow the signpost to the left of the road. The climb is stiff at first, but after about two miles turns into a gentle slope down to Glencoe, meeting the main road near Altnafeadh.

Serious climbing as practised in the Glencoe area is outside the scope of this book, but there are two modest scrambles which will give you something of the feeling of climbing without any great risks. It is possible to get a good way up the 3345 feet of Buachaille Etive Mór ('the great shepherd of Etive'), which dominates the eastern end of the glen, without undue exertion. It is a clear and straightforward path from Altnafeadh over the River Coupall. The final scramble up scree on to the ridge is optional! The second climb has as its objective the so-called 'Hidden Corrie', a rich upland pasture in which the Macdonalds are said to have concealed the cattle they stole from their neighbours. Its Gaelic name, Coire Gabhail ('the corrie of capture') seems to bear this story out. The path begins just to the west of the Meeting of Three Waters some three miles west of Altnafeadh, on the A82. It leads down to a wooden bridge across the River Coe (with hands as well as feet needed on the south side) and then up the right-hand side of the Allt Coire Gabhail. Where the gorge closes in, the path leads immediately above it, sloping outwards in places in a way that may put off beginners, especially if it is wet underfoot. An alternative route at this point, striking half-right away from the gorge, is squelchy but safer, and the path is picked up again after about half a mile. It then descends into the top of the gorge, crossing the stream and then disappearing among the massive boulders which, by damming the stream, have created the miniature alluvial plain of the corrie. The moment of entry to the corrie is truly dramatic; one second you are

Rannoch Moor

scrambling up the scree, and the next you are faced with a tranquil pasture. Certainly, if the legend of the Hidden Corrie is not true, it should be. To the left, about halfway down the corrie, is a spring of water that must be the most delicious in the world, and I always take a ritual swig.

So much for the pleasures of Glencoe. We must move on now from Kingshouse towards Tyndrum and Stirling. Continuing east from the hotel, a tarred roads leads to the A82, crosses it, and continues to the bottom of the ski lift. About halfway up is a mountaineering hut, Blackrock Cottage. Take the left fork here and, a little farther on, keep right where the road divides again. The true line of the military road is, in fact, about fifty yards up the mountainside, and can be easily seen in certain lights, but it is hardly worth twisted ankles for the sake of treading in soldiers' footprints. As the West Highland Way notice near Kingshouse warns, the next ten miles are exposed and remote, with very little in the way of shelter. This can be almost as much of a problem on a sunny day in

Blackrock Cottage and
Buachaille Etive Mór

Wade's road and Black Mount west of Bà Bridge

summer as in rain or fog, and in summer you would be well advised to have some cover for your head, as well as ample supplies of midge cream. As you rise across Black Mount, you begin to realize, on your left, the true awfulness of Rannoch Moor, with its evil-looking pools, and it is easy to imagine how travellers on the Glasgow to Fort William coach, which plied this route for some sixty years, must have looked upon it and shuddered. Beyond, however, the cone of Schiehallion rises serenely. In May, the Black Mount road skirts the snowline, with the newly released waters making caves out of the drifts. Also at this time of year you may see a blue or mountain hare (*Lepus timidus*) round about the snowline. On the ridge to the west, red deer may be seen and, in autumn, heard roaring. And then, about three miles from Blackrock Cottage, you will come down a long slope to find, set back a few yards from the road, Bà Cottage.

Opposite: Rannoch Moor

Bà Cottage is, in truth, no more than the ruin of a crofter's home

like thousands of others to be found in the Highlands, sad relics of the Clearances and of the triumph of sheep and deer over man. Yet it is possible here to reconstruct the whole way of life of its former occupants. You can still see the little path along which the women of the house went to the stream, the Allt Creagan nam Meann, for water, and the flat stones beside it on which they would have beaten out their washing. Beside the path is the distinct mound of a grave. Traditionally, Highland families buried their own dead, and in the northern Highlands still do. Whoever it is who is sleeping here beside the burn seems to have done better out of death than his descendants in the crematorium at Inverness or the cemetery at Fort William. It is true that the path to the stream has been kept alive by the campers who, despite the prohibitive notice at Kingshouse, continue to use this spot; but it is pleasant to think that they are keeping up a tradition (albeit unwittingly) that goes back centuries.

About half a mile farther on is Bà Bridge which, like all the bridges on this road, dates from Telford's improvements in the early years of the nineteenth century. From Kingshouse to Bridge of Orchy, this was the main road until 1932, when the new road fringing Rannoch Moor was laid, and towards Inveroran there are lengths of 1920s metalling still more or less intact. Shortly after the lochan beside the road about one mile beyond Bà Bridge, the military road strikes away to the right, running parallel with the Telford line about 500 yards up the slope. In patches, it can be traced easily enough, but it is hardly worth following and is, in any case, interrupted from time to time by forestry fencing. After running down alongside the Allt Chaorach, the older line and the newer one meet just north of Forest Lodge, and shortly after this, at Victoria Bridge, the road becomes metalled.

Drovers as well as soldiers came this way, and Inveroran, the settlement just beyond Victoria Bridge, was an important overnight stop. The Wordsworths stayed at the inn there (it was formerly a kingshouse, and is still a hotel), and Dorothy wrote a delightful cameo of the scene in the kitchen:

About seven or eight travellers, probably drovers, with as many dogs, were sitting in a complete circle round a large peat-fire in the middle of the floor, each with a mess of porridge, in a wooden vessel, upon his knee; a pot, suspended from one of the black beams, was boiling on the fire; two or three women pursuing their household business on the outside of the

Black Mount from Victoria Bridge

circle, children playing on the floor. There was nothing uncomfortable in this confusion: happy, busy or vacant faces, all looked pleasant; and even the smoky air, being a sort of natural indoor atmosphere of Scotland, served only to give a softening, I may say harmony, to the whole.

The cattle stance at Inveroran was the issue at stake in a hotly fought legal contest of the nineteenth century, when Lord Breadalbane, then the owner of the Black Mount estate, sought to close the Inveroran stance and replace it with one at Tyndrum. This would have made the drovers' march from the last stopping place, Altnafeadh, some eighteen miles, too long for a day's journey. The drovers successfully challenged Lord Breadalbane in the courts, but the decision was overruled by the House of Lords. In the end, it was agreed to establish a new stance at Achallader, at the opposite end of Loch Tulla, and indeed the site can still be seen from the Black Mount road between the A82 and the railway line.

The metalled road from Inveroran leads down to Bridge of Orchy, where there is another comfortable hotel with good drying facilities if you need them. There is also a railway station. It is one of the pleasant features of this walk that it can be adapted according to the amount of time in hand. It would be possible, for example, to drive to Fort William, leave your car there, walk to Kingshouse (a fairly strenuous twenty-mile slog), spend the night there, go on to Bridge of Orchy the next day (an easier ten miles or so) and either catch the

A forestry plough, near Bridge of Orchy

Near Bridge of Orchy

evening train back to Fort William or stay overnight and take the train that comes through about midday. Or you could dally at Kingshouse for a day or two and take some of my suggested excursions. Or alternatively you could walk on to Tyndrum and take the train there, or to Crianlarich and take it there. There are good hotels in both villages.

From the Bridge of Orchy Hotel the old road crosses the A82 and goes through the station subway under the West Highland Railway, to emerge as a track running parallel to the main road but far enough away for traffic noise not to intrude. After about two miles it crosses under the railway, which bears away left to follow the lower slopes of Beinn Dòrain and then to bridge the Auch Gleann by way of the famous Horseshoe Bend. The road takes a more direct course past Auch Farm, rejoining the railway and dodging to left and right of it until joins the A82 near the shop at Clifton. The West Highland Way signs lead up to the easternmost of Tyndrum's two stations,

Beinn Dòrain

Beinn Dòrain

where trains may be caught for Oban or Glasgow. (The other station serves Bridge of Orchy, the Rannoch Moor halts and Fort William.)

From here on, the military road peters out, largely overlaid by the A82, and the truth is that the best part of the walk is now behind you. However, the West Highland Way is amply marked from Tyndrum (not necessarily over military alignments) by thistle markers.

Of the roads that Caulfield initiated, as distinct from those he extended or improved, the road over Black Mount and the Devil's Staircase was probably the most important. It ran across country where both the people and the geography were hostile. There was no hope of billeting, so provisions and accommodation (mainly tented) had to travel with the men. It absorbed the labours of far above the usual numbers of men, partly because of the difficulties of supporting the working gangs. But, with some variations, it survived to serve Lochaber until well within living memory and, abandoned though it is now, deserves to be recognized as one of the roads that opened Scotland up.

8
The Lecht Road

Despite General Wade's strictures on the condition of the forts that he discovered when he took over command in Scotland in 1724, his efforts to strengthen them had remarkably little effect. As we have seen, Fort Augustus was crippled by one lucky shot, and Fort William escaped only by a whisker. On 2 February 1746 Wade's Fort George at Inverness was blown up by Prince Charles's artillery. It was, Burton says, 'little better than a great blockhouse' based on the old castle. The ease with which it was taken was a clear indication, after the event, that the policing and defence of the northern end of the Great Glen called for a more substantial cornerstone. The result of this was that in 1749 work was started on a new Fort George, designed to hold up to 3000 men, at Ardersier Point, some twelve miles east of Inverness. If Wade's forts had proved too puny, his successor intended to make no mistake on this occasion. There is only one word for the new Fort George: massive.

This shift of focus at the northern end of the Great Glen's defences led naturally to a reassessment of road communications. Even in Wade's time, some doubts had been expressed about the great Highland Road, and he is said to have planned a road from Ruthven to Braemar through Glen Feshie. This would have linked with the Minigaig Pass road from Calvine mentioned in Chapter 5, and cut out the long detour over Drumochter, as well as providing easier access to Aberdeen, which was used as a trooping port. The building of the new Fort George drew renewed attention to the virtues of a more easterly north–south route, and accordingly William Caulfield was ordered to survey a possible route from Perth to Inverness to run east of the mass of the Cairngorms.

He surveyed the route in 1748 and work began the following year on parts of the southern section, northwards from Blairgowrie and between Spittal of Glenshee and Braemar. After that – perhaps because of the competitive claims of the road across the Devil's Staircase and the Black Mount – there seems to have been a pause

Garnshiel Lodge

until the spring of 1753, when the the gangs began work between Braemar and Corgarff and also towards the Well of the Lecht. The Lecht road was continued in 1754 and in the following year the whole road to Fort George was completed.

About a hundred miles long, this was the last substantial military road to be built in Scotland. The sense of urgency that had attended the road-building programme under Wade had passed, and in any case shrewd observers may have noted that Wade's roads had, in the Forty-Five, proved of rather more assistance to the rebels than to the occupying forces. After the departure of Prince Charles and the merciless pursuit of his supporters by the Duke of Cumberland, it seemed unlikely that heart – or indeed men – could be found for a further rebellion. As for England's role as the occupying power, it became progressively less military in its stance and took other, more effective forms, mainly economic. Certainly, economic activity demanded good communications, and as we have seen the military   *Hill of Allargue*

Garnshiel Lodge

roads were not always easily adaptable to civilian purposes; but an attack on economic needs would have to wait until the Commissioners for Highland Roads and Bridges were established in 1803. The most important factor in the tailing-off of the military road programme was, however, its escalating cost. The system of funding in the early days was simply to charge costs to the Army, which recovered them by adding them to next year's precept. This was not a system likely to encourage thrift, and if work had to be suspended in a bad season it could make the cost of the whole enterprise dauntingly high. Later, Parliament insisted on seeing estimates in advance, but this did not greatly improve matters and the apparent extravagance of the road scheme continued to worry the government. General Mackay, Commander of the Forces in Scotland in the 1780s, complained that 'no regular system seems to have been laid down in carrying on this business', and this view would have found many supporters in London. The fact was that the military roads, especially Wade's early ones, had become a burden. The authorities had underestimated the need for maintenance, had miscalculated the dire effects of the Scottish winter, and had perhaps placed too much faith in the building techniques used by Wade and Caulfield. The calculation of the stresses likely to be placed on bridges in times of spate, for example, seem to have been fairly hit or miss, with the result that some bridges were simply torn away in the spring floods. Others needed extensive repair or rebuttressing.

Caulfield died in 1767 and so was spared the criticisms of Mackay and others of the work which had occupied virtually all his working life. By 1780 the maintenance of the roads had become a matter of patching the worst stretches, and some of them were by then being described as 'ruinous'. From about 1790 soldiers ceased to be employed on maintenance work, and civilian gangs were used instead. Some roads were simply allowed to rot; the Highbridge to Melgarve road (Chapter 6) may have been one of them.

The Fort George road south of Grantown-on-Spey was not among the roads taken over by the Commissioners for Highland

Near the Well of Lecht

Corgarff Castle

Roads and Bridges. This meant that from 1814 onwards its upkeep was in the hands of local landowners and the shire authorities, whose degree of interest and investment was very variable. It also means that there is a greater variety of bridges than usual, which is perhaps one of the reasons why the road has quite a different feel from the others in this book.

After 1745, the English forces began to concern themselves more closely than before in the fight against cattle-thieving, which had always been a Highland problem but now threatened to become an epidemic. The Lecht road, lying across the path of stolen droves from Banffshire, was to play a part in this plan, and Corgarff Castle, originally a hunting lodge belonging to the Earls of Mar, was bought by the government in 1746 and refortified for use by a garrison whose main purpose was to control the theft of cattle, not, it must be said, with any great success.

The drive up the A93 from Blairgowrie through Glen Shee is a

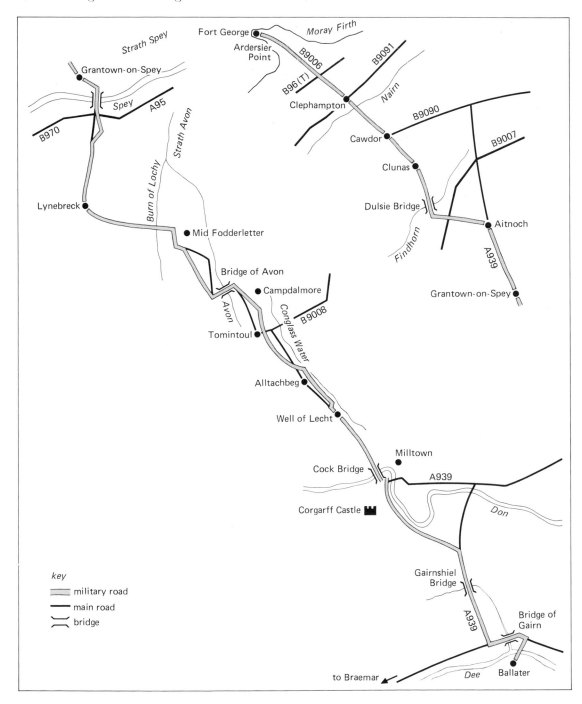

good introduction to the road, though it tends to be busy in summer with Braemar-bound holiday traffic. I am going to suggest that you start walking at Ballater, heading north on what is now the A939 through Bridge of Gairn. There are only minor deviations between the original line and the present one until, some four miles beyond Gairnshiel Bridge, the old road bears northwest to avoid crossing the River Don, keeping to the left bank past Corgarff Castle as far as Milltown. It is necessary to take the newer crossing of the Don by Cock Bridge on the A939, and now we are on the Lecht road proper. Ahead is a climb to cross the watershed at 2114 feet, which is achieved in two miles of pretty exhausting going, and it is this climb that – together with the road's exposure to the weather – has given the Lecht road its fearsome reputation. The road was greatly feared in the nineteenth century, and although it was designed for use by carriages, only the most steel-nerved of passengers attempted it.

Original and modern road run together to the Well of the Lecht, where a stone on the left, above the parking area, records the construction of the Lecht road 'from here to the Spey' in 1754 by five companies of the 33rd Regiment under Colonel Lord Charles Hay. In his report of 1750, William Caulfield expressed the gravest doubts about the road from the Lecht northwards as far as the Spey, which, he said, 'mostly run through moors and spongy ground and will require many ditches and side drains and will take full 800 men to make this road in one season.' (In fact, as we have seen, the work was split over several years.) Caulfield went on to warn that this road 'though ever so well made' would soon be destroyed unless local people stopped their practice of dragging timber along it, 'tearing away the gravel and making channels for the rain water, which thus gathers into currents and destroys all before them.' The movement of timber was, in fact, one of the great problems of Highland road-builders. More than one bridge was weakened and finally destroyed by floating timber down the rivers. Even if it was carted along the roads, the carts – unusually heavy loads for that time – made ruts which themselves became watercourses. It was a problem not finally solved until the railways disposed of it.

Caulfield's line follows the A939 as far as the outskirts of Tomintoul, with one exception about one mile from the Well of the Lecht where the present road runs under an embankment while Caulfield's line is above. Crossing Conglass Water to follow its left

Commemorative stone,
Well of Lecht

bank, the road continues to Alltachbeg, where Caulfield's line forks to the left to enter Tomintoul past the church. Tomintoul's claim to distinction (and possibly a dubious one) is that, at 1160 feet, it is the highest village in the Highlands. This did not impress Queen Victoria, who noted, after a visit in 1860, that it was 'the most tumbledown, poor-looking place I ever saw'. The judgement seems harsh. There was a further diversion at the northern end of the village, not now walkable, where Caulfield followed the line of the present drive to Campdalmore and then swung left to the Bridge of Avon. Just after the bridge, where the A939 turns sharply right, Caulfield went straight on on a track that is still traceable, emerging after about half a mile just short of the turning to Mid Fodderletter. Another short diversion occurs beyond Lynebreck, after a spectacular and seemingly never-ending four miles, where the Caulfield road skirted an escarpment to the left, and then crossed over to the right of the A939 for about half a mile. The entry to Grantown-on-Spey, over a splendid three-arched bridge now used by pedestrians only

Near Fodderletter

*Near Lynemore, looking
north to Grantown*

Opposite:
Bridge of Brown

and superseded for road traffic by a modern structure, is unmistakable.

Grantown-on-Spey is the end of the best walking on this road, and the end of the Lecht section, but if you are interested in following Caulfield to Fort George (which is best done by car) take the A939 out of Grantown as far as Aitnoch. Here, take a left turn along a minor road for Dulsie Bridge and Clunas, and follow the signs for Cawdor, where the B9090 is joined. Turn left to go through Cawdor village and on to Clephampton, from where a virtually straight B9006 takes you to Fort George.

Bibliography

James Boswell, *A Tour to the Hebrides with Samuel Johnson, LL.D.*, Heinemann, 1936.

John Malcolm Bulloch, *Old Highland Highways*, Robert Carruthers & Son, Inverness, 1931.

Edward Burt, *Letters from a Gentleman in the North of Scotland*, Rest Fenner, London, 1818.

John Hill Burton, *The History of Scotland*, William Blackwood & Sons, Edinburgh, 1880.

R. Carruthers, *The Highland Notebook, 1841*, Adam & Charles Black, Edinburgh, 1843.

Margaret Forster, *The Rash Adventurer: The Rise and Fall of Charles Edward Stuart*, Secker & Warburg, 1973.

F. Fraser Darling and J. Morton Boyd, *The Highlands and Islands*, Collins, revised edition, 1969.

A. R. B. Haldane, *The Drove Roads of Scotland*, Nelson, 1952.

A. R. B. Haldane, *New Ways through the Glens*, Nelson, 1962.

D. G. Moir, *Scottish Hill Tracks: Northern Scotland*, John Bartholemew & Son, Edinburgh, revised edition, 1975.

Murray's *Handbook for Scotland*, John Murray, 1894.

National Trust for Scotland, *Glencoe and Dalness*, National Trust for Scotland, Edinburgh, n.d.

John Prebble, *Culloden*, Secker & Warburg, 1961.

John Prebble, *Glencoe*, Secker & Warburg, 1966.

J. B. Salmond, *Wade in Scotland*, The Moray Press, Edinburgh, 1938.

T. C. Smout, *A History of the Scottish People 1560–1830*, Collins, 1969.

William Taylor, *The Military Roads in Scotland*, David and Charles, Newton Abbot, 1976.

Derick S. Thomson and Ian Grimble, *The Future of the Highlands*, Routledge & Kegan Paul, 1968.

Katherine Tomasson and Francis Buist, *Battles of the '45*, Batsford, 1962.

David Turnock (ed.), *Patterns of Highland Development*, Macmillan, 1970.

Charles Richard Weld, *Two Months in the Highlands, Orcadia and Skye*, William Blackwood & Sons, Edinburgh, 1903.

James Wilson, *A Voyage Round the Coasts of Scotland and the Isles*, Adam & Charles Black, Edinburgh, 1847.

Dorothy Wordsworth, *Recollections of a Tour made in Scotland A.D.1803*, Edmonston and Douglas, Edinburgh, 1874.

A.J. Youngson, *After the Forty-Five*, Edinburgh University Press, Edinburgh, 1973.

Index